TEMPLARS AND HOSPITALLERS

MEDIEVAL INSTITUTE

University of Notre Dame

The Conway Lectures in Medieval Studies
2008

The Medieval Institute gratefully acknowledges the generosity of Robert M. Conway and his support for the lecture series and publications resulting from it.

PREVIOUS TITLES IN THIS SERIES:

Paul Strohm
Politique: Languages of Statecraft between Chaucer and Shakespeare (2005)

Ulrich Horst, O.P.
The Dominicans and the Pope: Papal Teaching Authority in the Medieval and Early Modern Thomist Tradition (2006)

Rosamond McKitterick
Perceptions of the Past in the Early Middle Ages (2006)

TEMPLARS

AND

HOSPITALLERS

as Professed Religious in the Holy Land

JONATHAN RILEY-SMITH

University of Notre Dame Press

Notre Dame, Indiana

Copyright © 2010 by the University of Notre Dame Press
Notre Dame, Indiana 46556
www.undpress.nd.edu
All Rights Reserved

Manufactured in the United States of America

Library of Congress Cataloging-in-Publication Data

Riley-Smith, Jonathan Simon Christopher, 1938–
    Templars and Hospitallers as professed religious in the Holy Land /
Jonathan Riley-Smith.
        p.   cm. — (The Conway lectures in medieval studies)
    Includes bibliographical references and index.
    ISBN-13: 978-0-268-04058-1 (pbk. : alk. paper)
    ISBN-10: 0-268-04058-3 (pbk. : alk. paper)
    1. Templars—History—To 1500.   2. Hospitalers—History—To 1500.
3. Military religious orders—History.   4. Mediterranean Region—History—
476–1517.   I. Title.
    CR4743.R55   2009
    271'.7913—dc22

                                                                2009035058

CONTENTS

PREFACE

I began to work on the Military Orders nearly half a century ago, when my research supervisor at Cambridge, R. C. Smail, provided me with a wonderful topic. Beginners need projects that everyone agrees ought to be undertaken and for which the materials are easily available. The activities in the Latin East of the Order of the Hospital of St John of Jerusalem badly needed re-examination. Most of the archival material had been published around 1900 in a four-volume *Cartulaire général*, and the only serious monograph had been published at about the same time. The history of the kingdom of Jerusalem, where the order had its headquarters, had been transformed in the 1950s by the researches of Jean Richard in France and Joshua Prawer in Israel.

Once the PhD dissertation had turned itself into a book I moved on to other topics, although I continued to publish occasional pieces on the Hospitallers. In the late 1990s, feeling that the time had come for me to concentrate on the Military Orders once again, I began to look closely at the Templars, with the intention of writing a book on their order as a religious one. Illness intervened, but when an invitation arrived from the University of Notre Dame to deliver the Robert M. Conway Lectures I thought it might be useful to put together the work I had done over the years in a comparative study of the Templars and Hospitallers as professed brothers of orders of the Church stationed in the Levant. I have rearranged some of the material in the lectures for the purposes of publication.

I would like to thank the Medieval Institute of the University of Notre Dame, and Professors Thomas Noble and Olivia Remie Constable, for their invitation and their hospitality. I am grateful to Barbara Hanrahan and Matthew Dowd of the University of Notre Dame Press for their support and efficiency.

Cambridge
J. S. C. R-S.

ABBREVIATIONS

AOL   *Archives de l'Orient Latin*

Cart Hosp   *Cartulaire général de l'ordre des Hospitaliers*, ed. Delaville Le Roulx

CCCM   *Corpus Christianorum, Continuatio Medievalis*

MGHS   *Monumenta Germaniae Historica Scriptores in Folio et Quarto*, ed. Georg H. Pertz et al., 39 vols so far (Hanover and Leipzig, 1826–).

PL   *Patrologiae Cursus Completus. Series Latina*, comp. Jacques P. Migne, 217 vols and 4 vols of indexes (Paris, 1841–64).

Procès   *Le procès des Templiers*, ed. Michelet

QFIAB   *Quellen und Forschungen aus italienischen Archiven und Bibliotheken*

RHC   *Recueil des historiens des croisades*, ed. Académie des Inscriptions et Belles Lettres (Paris, 1841–1906).

RHC Oc   *RHC Historiens occidentaux*, 5 vols (Paris, 1844–95).

ROL   *Revue de l'Orient Latin*

Templar and Hospitaller Communities in the Levant

PROLOGUE

Military Orders are orders of the Roman Catholic Church, the brothers (and occasionally sisters) of which are professed religious, subject to the usual obligations of, and constraints in, canon law, except that some of them had the right and duty to bear arms. Priests are forbidden by canon law to use force and these orders were—one of them still is—unusual in that they were run by their unordained brothers.[1] Many flourished in the central Middle Ages, engaged in warfare not only in the eastern Mediterranean region but also along the shores of the Baltic and in the Iberian Peninsula. They ranged from international corporations, such as the Temple and the much smaller St Lazarus, to regional ones, such as the Iberian Orders of Calatrava, Aviz, Santiago, Alcántara, Christ and Montesa, the German Brothers of the Sword and Knights of Dobrzyn, and the tiny English Order of St Thomas. Only two, the Hospital of St John of Jerusalem (now known as the Sovereign Military Order of Malta) and the Order of St Mary of the Germans (the Teutonic Order), survive today as orders of the Church, although they are no longer military in practice. The priests of the Teutonic Order run parishes, and the members of the Order of Malta care for the sick poor.[2]

Military Orders are to be distinguished from Secular and Christian Orders of Chivalry. Secular Orders of Chivalry are subject not to the Church and canon law (except in so far as their members are baptized Christians) but to the sovereignty of their princely founders

1

and their constitutional or dynastic successors. They acquire legitimi-
zation, therefore, not through the recognition of them as religious orders by the Church, but through the acts of secular Founts of Honours.
Their knights are not such through profession but by virtue of the ac-
tion of a sovereign power or its successor, and although it was common
for some private devotional obligations to be imposed on them their role
was, and is, honorific. As one of their most recent historians has written, "The only goal common to [these orders] was the promotion and
reward of loyal service."[3]

Christian Orders of Chivalry evolved out of the Iberian Military
Orders, the secularization of which by the Spanish and Portuguese
kings was underway from the fifteenth century.[4] In a few cases, however, the secularization was only partial because elements from the past
were retained for a significant period of time. The resulting hybrids
were no longer orders of the Church, since they had become confraternities legitimized by secular Founts of Honours, but their membership
continued, unlike Secular Orders of Chivalry, to entail public, as opposed to private, obligations relating to the defence of Christendom or
the Faith. Their knights—particularly those of Santiago and Christ—
continued to serve in North Africa or in Mediterranean galley fleets or
in the Portuguese empire.[5] They were the models for other Christian
Orders of Chivalry—in Italy, France, Germany, Holland, and Britain—
that were established between the sixteenth century and the end of the
nineteenth.[6]

— This book is concerned with the members of the two earliest and
most famous Military Orders and with their service in Palestine and
Syria in the central Middle Ages.[7] Much has been written about them—
indeed it could be said that they have never been as popular with re-
searchers as they are today—but historians have tended to concentrate
on them as military phenomena, international institutions, economic
powerhouses, and landowners.[8] Very little attention has been paid
to their primary role as religious orders.[9] They make no appearance
in Cottineau's great inventory of monastic and religious houses,[10] al-

though they were added, at Neville Hadcock's insistence, to Dom David Knowles's gazetteer of medieval English religious communities.[11] A striking example of unconscious neglect was a recent PhD dissertation on the veneration of St John the Baptist in England, which was outstanding, but which did not recognize the significance of the many commanderies of the Hospitallers of St John.

The Hospital and the Temple were endowed with estates throughout Europe, where their leading representatives were often major figures in the kingdoms in which they resided. They were used extensively by the papacy in the promotion of crusades and the collection of crusade taxes. Their more articulate contemporaries, who subjected them to quite severe criticism[12] and in the late thirteenth century debated how they could be merged,[13] appear at first reading to have believed that they were very similar to one another, but I will try to explain why this impression, which has helped to fashion almost all the history written about them, is a false one. A theme of this book is that they had distinct personalities, formed by the purposes for which they had been founded. The Templars had one over-riding goal. The Hospitallers had several.

The source material for their history is rich. Many of the documents generated by the Hospitallers in Palestine and Syria have survived, together with a substantial body of statutory legislation, case law, and custom.[14] The Templars' central archive, on the other hand, has almost entirely disappeared, although it may have been in Europe in the fifteenth century,[15] and their statutes, enacted in Levantine chapters-general, very few of the meetings of which can be identified,[16] survive only in summary form, incorporated in a code which was built up layer upon layer over the years.[17]

In one respect, however, the Temple provides us with material that is more revealing than anything that is associated with the Hospital. On 13 October 1307 most of the brothers in the kingdom of France, including the grand master James of Molay, who had come from Cyprus on a visitation, were arrested and accused of blasphemy, idolatry, and heresy. The Church's response was to set up investigations, the earliest group of which comprises an examination by the papal inquisitor in

Paris, some episcopal enquiries, and depositions made before the pope at Poitiers and a team of cardinals at Chinon in the summer of 1308.[18] These were followed by a string of others,[19] including a papal commission which was sitting in Paris from 1309 to 1311.[20] The testimony of individual Templars recorded during the interrogations provides us with details about their careers and with glimpses of the situation in Palestine and Syria during the last thirty years of western occupation.

— I shall be concentrating on the activities of the two orders in the Levant, but it should never be forgotten that from the middle of the twelfth century the bulk of their membership at any given time was running their estates in the West. The resources their central convents (or headquarters), situated in Jerusalem before 1187 and in Acre on the Palestinian coast from the 1190s to 1291, needed in manpower, cash, and matériel could only come from these lands, and there is ample evidence for the relative efficiency with which they managed their vast property portfolios[21] and for the systems of communication that enabled them to direct eastwards the income they derived from them. The brothers in Europe lived a community life in commanderies (or preceptories), which were gathered into provinces called priories by the Hospitallers and grand commanderies or provincial masterships by the Templars. The provinces could be grouped into even larger circumscriptions, managed by Hospitaller grand commanders of *outremer* (a word which in this case meant Europe) and by Templar masters *deçà mer* or visitors-general. The provinces and commanderies themselves generated masses of archival material and it is not surprising that their economic roles have been at the forefront of the minds of many of the historians who have written about them.

The orders' hunger for cash drove them to turn themselves into the first true orders of the Church. These have supranational, or rather supradiocesan, structures. The brothers and sisters, wherever they are, share the same privileges, including that of exemption which liberates them from the powers of local bishops; the same regular life; and the same obedience to a common central authority, which can transfer them from place to place. It is true that other congregations of religious evolved in the eleventh and twelfth centuries, but none of them initially showed the features of a true order. Either the monks, wherever they were, pretended to be where they were not, so that a Cluniac monk at an overseas priory was treated as if he was within the walls of a virtual abbey, located at Cluny in Burgundy, or there was a confederation of independent abbeys, like the Cistercian ones.

The chief reason for the precocity of the Military Orders was that they were institutions that had to focus not on some geographically convenient location within Europe but on the eastern fringe of Christendom. Their headquarters were therefore dependent on resources that were being generated a long way away from them. The early stage at which they began to evolve intermediate government suggests that they had been forced to delegate. There was no obvious model for them to follow, and their provincial representatives had to work out through trial and error a means of controlling scattered dependencies. The first Hospitaller provincial chapter can be found meeting in 1123, and by the 1160s the terms of the relationship between the local houses and the provincial heads in both orders was becoming clear.[22] The structures the Hospitallers and Templars were establishing were to be the models for later religious orders, including those of the Franciscans and Dominicans.

The brothers in the East must always have been conscious of a western hinterland that was a source not only of income and supplies, but also of fresh blood and possibly new ideas.[23] Most of them had been born and raised in Europe and many of them would return there for a period of service or for good. As members of religious orders they were dependent on, and ultimately answerable to, the popes in Italy; and committed as they were to the defence of the settlements in the east and, in the case of the Hospital, to the care of pilgrims, they knew that the flow to them of resources was subject to the moods of western rulers and to the arbitrary nature of political developments in the west. It is not surprising that their leaders took the trouble to correspond regularly and informatively with European rulers,[24] but they were usually impotent in the face of events over which they had little control.

Master Hugh Revel of the Hospital wrote bitterly in 1268 of the dire effects European political disturbances were having on his order's income. He described how an unauthorized armed contribution made by Philip of Egly, the Hospitaller prior of France, to Charles of Anjou's cause in southern Italy, had swallowed up the order's revenues in Italy and Apulia and had left the priory of France itself deeply in debt. Hospitaller properties in Sicily and Tuscany had been devastated. Elsewhere, civil war in England had drastically reduced the value of its priory's *responsions*, the levy on the order's houses that helped fund the central convent. The Iberian Peninsula had contributed nothing except some mules, and the priories of Auvergne and St Gilles and the bailiwick of Germany had sent less than expected.[25]

It was essential, as we shall see, that some of the most able brothers be put into positions of responsibility in the West. But in spite of the wars and periods of insecurity, life in rural and even urban communities in Europe must have been less stressful than that of the brothers in the East and it may have been the case that the norms of religious community existence could be followed more closely in relatively peaceful locations in France and Italy. It cannot be denied that against one contemporary measure of success—a reputation for holiness—the Templar and Hospitaller communities in the Levant performed poorly. Both orders were credited with remarkably few saints in an age when in the eyes of the faithful heaven was filling up with men and women belonging to the new religious orders. And, of the three holy men associated with the Temple—Everard of Barres, Bevignate, and Gerland[26]—and (after putting to one side those saints who were fabricated or appropriated from elsewhere) the four in the modern calendar of the Sovereign Military Order of Malta—the founder Gerard, Ubaldesca, Toscana, and Hugh of Genoa[27]—only three, or possibly four, were full members of their respective orders, and only two of those who were order members appear to have served in the East. Of course, it may have been that the cults of brothers once known in the Levant for their piety were forgotten once their graves could no longer be visited.[28] Who now hears of St William, a local Latin bishop, or St Eudes, a count of Nevers, whose tombs were healing shrines in Acre in the thirteenth century?[29]

But although the evidence is slight, life in the European houses could have provided the brothers and sisters with more intellectual and spiritual stimulus than was possible in the threatened convents on the frontiers. It came to be believed that the Hospitaller priest Hugh's record of prayerful service to the sick in Genoa demonstrated that while the brothers in the East fought the Muslims, their *confrères* in the West supported them by engaging in their own spiritual battles "against invisible enemies."[30]

Chapter One

THE ESTABLISHMENT
OF TRADITIONS

In March 1198 there was a gathering in Acre of almost everyone of importance in the city. The patriarch of Jerusalem; the archbishops of Nazareth, Tyre and Caesarea; the bishops of Bethlehem and Acre; the masters of the Temple and the Hospital; Henry of Champagne, the ruler of the kingdom of Jerusalem; the lords of Tiberias, Sidon, and Caesarea; and John of Ibelin, the half brother of Henry's wife, the heiress to the kingdom, were joined by leading German crusaders, who were soon to return home. They resolved to ask Pope Innocent III to allow a German field hospital, which had been set up during the Third Crusade eight years before, to add the exercise of arms to its nursing duties. They suggested that it "should have the regulations of the Hospital of St John concerning the sick and the poor, as in the past, but for the rest should have the rule of the knighthood of the Temple with respect to clerics, knights and other brothers." Innocent agreed that the new institution, the Teutonic Order, should follow "the practice of the Temple with respect to clerics and knights and the example of the Hospitallers with respect to the poor and the sick."[1]

If the Hospitallers had had their way, the Teutonic Order would have been strangled at birth. They had tried to prevent it setting itself up in Acre on the grounds that the papacy had granted them the sole right to care for the sick in the city.[2] Convinced that the German hospital was a continuation of a dependency they had managed in Jerusalem, they fought unsuccessfully to establish their jurisdiction over it. At any rate, it is clear that the founders of the Teutonic Order, who included the pope, the ecclesiastical and secular rulers of the kingdom of Jerusalem, and the Templar and Hospitaller masters themselves, recognized that the Temple and the Hospital had different missions.

The Origins of the Temple and Its Ethos

In the euphoria that had swept the west after the Christian occupation of Jerusalem a century earlier a number of European knights had committed themselves to the defence of the new settlement. They had attached themselves to churches in and around the city, adopting a form of association not unlike those that lay *confratres* had with religious houses in Europe. Although by the thirteenth century several different accounts of the origins of the Templars were in circulation,[3] the one that has been generally accepted is that a few of these knights, who had chosen to serve the church of the Holy Sepulchre, formed themselves into a brotherhood, with the aim of securing the pilgrim roads to and from the Holy Places, the perilous nature of which had been highlighted the previous Easter when a large party of pilgrims had lost hundreds of their number on the desert journey between Jerusalem and the Jordan. The leader of the new fraternity was a petty noble from Champagne or Burgundy called Hugh of Payns.[4]

If this is really what happened, the decision must have been made in the late autumn of 1119, at a time when the western settlers were also transfixed by the news of the annihilation of a Christian army in northern Syria. The company of knights took vows of poverty, celibacy, and obedience. Its initiative was approved by the patriarch of Jerusalem and was recognized at a church council, which met in Nablus in January 1120 and agreed to a canon legitimating the bearing of arms by churchmen.[5] King Baldwin II of Jerusalem, who was notoriously mean, lent it part of one of his residences, the al-Aqsa mosque on the

Temple esplanade, which was in a ruinous state.[6] Financial support was assured by a levy which seems to have been agreed to by—or was imposed on—some of the religious houses in Jerusalem, because the canons of the Holy Sepulchre were providing the Templars with an annual subvention of 150 besants, "for the defence of the land," until it was exchanged for three villages in the 1160s,[7] and the Hospitallers' contribution of the left-overs from their conventual table was only redeemed by their master in the 1240s.[8]

The potential value of a permanent military commitment, which could supplement the less reliable and spasmodic contribution of visiting knights, must have been clear to everyone. Count Fulk V of Anjou, who happened to be in Palestine on crusade, was closely associated with Hugh of Payns and his companions within months of their foundation[9] and his support must have encouraged the first benefactions in Europe. Bernard of Clairvaux, who belonged to the same Champenois-Burgundian circle of families as did Hugh, persuaded a papal legate and the archbishops, bishops and abbots attending a council at Troyes in 1129 to recognize the new society and approve a Rule, which was the first in the history of the Church to try to reconcile the regular life with the bearing of arms.[10]

The formation and reception of the Templar ideal are well documented. The promulgation of the Rule was followed by a letter addressed to the brothers by a man called Hugh, who could have been their first master,[11] although it may never have reached its audience and was anyway forgotten; by a letter of encouragement and penitential advice to Hugh of Payns from Guigo, the prior of La Grande Chartreuse, who wished the "holy knighthood" success in both physical and spiritual warfare;[12] by Pope Innocent II's charter of privilege, *Omne datum optimum*;[13] and by Bernard of Clairvaux's defence of their way of life, *De laude novae militiae*.[14] In the later thirteenth century the brother knight Gerald of Gaûche had his own copy of *De laude* while serving in the East,[15] and the cords worn by the brothers, which seem to have been similar to scapulars, were said to have been adopted in honour, or at the command, of Bernard, who some even believed to have been their founder.[16]

The authors of these early texts portrayed the Templars as men who had dedicated their lives "to carrying arms in defence of Christians against the enemies of the faith and on behalf of peace."[17] Members of an entirely new kind of order, theologically justifiable, in which knighthood and the religious life were conjoined,[18] they expressed in their actions love of God and of their neighbour, for whom they were prepared to lay down their lives.

> Like true Israelites and warriors most versed in holy battle [wrote Pope Innocent], on fire with the flame of true love, you carry out in your deeds the words of the Gospel, in which it is said *Greater love than this no man hath, that a man lay down his life for his friends.*[19]

As professed knights of Christ, prayerful, dedicated, disciplined, ascetic, and ready to seek martyrdom in imitation of their Savior, they outshone their secular counterparts, whose way of life was as dangerous for their souls as it was for their bodies.[20]

The knighthood described in this material was the antithesis of chivalry, as it was to be later understood. Chivalry was in many respects a secular parody of Christianity, with its own scriptures, liturgy and iconography. Although Hugh and his companions must have shared the predilections of the society into which they had been born and of western lay confraternities, of one of which, of course, they had been members, they rejected in the strongest terms the secular world's trappings and many of its values. Their imagery was biblical and their language was theological. Templar knighthood was rooted in monastic history, since it picked up, and ran with, the transference to physical warfare of the monastic ideal of the knight of Christ, which was already being expressed in crusade literature.[21] The First Crusade had popularized the new idea that fighting in a good cause with a right intention could be an act of penance, and monastic commentators had drawn attention to the gulf that was opening up between secular warrior reprobates and crusading knights of Christ. In an example of the way their instincts as Church reformers led them to monasticize the temporal world around them, they had portrayed the crusade as a nomadic fighting monastery in which the temporarily professed performed penitential service.[22] The Templars—who, as Thomas Aquinas suggested with reference to all the Military Orders a century and a half later, could not have come into existence without the concept of penitential warfare[23]—made the short-term service of a crusader permanent and enveloped it in liturgical prayer. It was this feature of their ethos that attracted contemplatives like Guigo of La Grande Chartreuse and Bernard of Clairvaux himself. William Purkis has recently argued cogently that Bernard transferred from crusading to the Templars the idea that an individual imitated in his or her actions those of Christ. For Bernard and others the crusade remained a means by which a pious layman could gain spiritual reward, but only by profession into the Temple could the life of a warrior become one that was truly modelled on Christ.[24]

The radical nature of the Templars' mission was highlighted in Pope Innocent's extraordinary concession that the brother priests in the order should be subordinated to the authority of the brother knights,[25] at a time when the advance of priestly prestige must have been considered to be unstoppable. It is almost impossible to find the words to express how absolute the Templar commitment to the specialized role of fighting for Christendom was supposed to be and how melodramatically it was expressed in sober behavior and in bearing. It was famously symbolized by the brothers' bearded faces. When in Jacquemart Gielee's late-thirteenth-century satirical epic, *Renart le Nouvel,* the fox decided to assume the mastership of both the Hospital and the Temple he promised that his clothing would be divided.

> On my right side I will wear the habit of a Hospitaller and on my left that of a Templar; I will leave the left side of my face bearded and I will shave the right.[26]

It is striking how often in the accounts of the early-fourteenth-century interrogations there are references to brothers who had shaved off their beards to mark their abandonment of the order.[27]

The Templar ideal was such a departure from Christian tradition that of course there were churchmen who were upset by it. One of the most severe of the early critics was Abbot Isaac of l'Etoile, who in a sermon preached between 1147 and 1169 fulminated against what he described—in a swipe at his confrère Bernard of Clairvaux—as both a *nova militia* and a *monstrum novum.*

> They lawfully despoil and religiously kill those who do not know the name of Christ and they proclaim their own men, who perish in these massacres, to be martyrs of Christ.[28]

Isaac was not unusual in his dislike of the notion of the warrior martyr, which was so important to Templar self-identity. The Church was always uncomfortable with the idea, however often its senior representatives might generalize hyperbolically about it, and specific references to the martyrdom of members of the Military Orders were rare in the central Middle Ages.[29] The Cistercians seem to have preserved the memory of Templars martyred after the fall of the castle of Vadum Jacob to Saladin in 1179,[30] and the Franciscans, together with the Templars themselves, were convinced that the defenders of the castle of Saphet, who were massacred by the Egyptians in 1266, were also martyrs.[31] But the martyrdoms in the second case—and probably in both—were of a conventional sort involving the refusal of captives to apostatize.

In other ways, however, Isaac was not representative. Root-and-branch critics like him were always to be in a small minority. Most Latin Christians considered the Templars' mission to be a valuable one and supported it with benefactions, at least until the late thirteenth century, when public opinion was turning against the Military Orders—and particularly the Temple—believing them to have been chiefly responsible for the loss of the last Christian outposts in the Holy Land.

Approval was rarely unconditional, however. Even those who considered the Templars' role to be justifiable and useful tended to be in two minds about it, because they knew that muscular Christianity could all too easily lead to worldliness, vainglory, and competitiveness, the very attributes of secular knighthood that the Templars claimed to have renounced. They, like the Hospitallers, must have heard a homily every Sunday after the conventual Mass,[32] and two sermons, preached to them by James of Vitry, bishop of Acre and later cardinal, and honed by him for presentation as exemplars to a wider public, give some indication of the opinions of a senior churchman in the early thirteenth century. James praised and justified the Templar way of life, but in the first sermon he warned the brothers at length against pride in birth, wealth or power, anger, envy, greed, quarrelsomeness, and secular habits—"He is a miserable man who thinks of his horse more than of Christ"[33]—and he ended the second with an anecdote that he set in the early years, when, as he acerbically put it, "the brothers were still poor and fervent in religion."[34] The anxieties he voiced were to be more strongly expressed by others—and with respect to the Hospital as well—as the years went by.

Features of the Templar ideal nevertheless remained dedication to the specialized role of professed Christian knighthood, the love perceived to be expressed in it, and the gulf that separated the brothers from their worldly contemporaries.[35] They were passed on to all the Military Orders and were strong enough to survive until the end of the eighteenth century.[36] In the case of the Hospital, however, they were modified.[37]

THE EARLY HISTORY OF THE HOSPITAL

The origins of the Hospital predated those of the Temple. A hospice or hospital for pilgrims was established in ca. 1080 by the only Latin institution at that time in Muslim Jerusalem, the Benedictine abbey of St Mary. The hospital's independence of the abbey was confirmed by Pope Paschal II in 1113. It has been suggested that until the Hospitallers composed their own Rule, perhaps twenty years later, they comprised a lay community,[38] but Paschal himself referred to them as *fratres professi*,[39] and a Rule was not a requirement for a religious institute to be authentic. The Carthusians did not have a Rule. St Francis did not want one. It is likely that the nucleus of the new society was made up of Benedictine *fratres conversi* (serving brothers). These men were establishing, in Kaspar Elm's phrase, a "self-standing order of *conversi*,"[40] which must have provided the model a few years later for the founders of the Temple, who of course had different aims.

Inspired by the injunction to behave towards each person as though he or she was Christ himself, the early Hospitallers imagined a fictional relationship in which they were serfs or slaves and the "holy poor" were their lords, or, in other words, their proprietors. They made their ideal a reality by ministering to poor pilgrims when they were sick and burying them when they died,[41] but the first evidence for an embryonic military wing is to be found as early as 1126, only six years after the foundation of the Temple, and the custody of a major castle was entrusted to them ten years later.[42] By the 1140s the order's military contribution seems to have been making it more attractive to richer nobles, who began to appear in its ranks,[43] and the class of brothers-at-arms must have been quite numerous by the 1160s because a report sent to Rome suggests that they were already occupying many of the major offices[44] and because the design of the castle of Belvoir, begun at that time, allowed for a large conventual enclosure.

The adoption of military functions by an institution that had been established for a very different purpose was in its way as radical a step as that taken in the foundation of the Temple. "Folk-memories" of the process, preserved in two versions written around 1500, suggest that secular knights, who like the original Templars had come to the East to serve for a few years out of piety or for pay and had attached themselves to the Hospital, were incorporated to form a military class.[45] I have not found any contemporary evidence for para-crusading knights serving the Hospital at an early date,[46] but their needs would explain references from the 1120s to arms-bearers in the West leaving their horses and weapons to the Hospital in their wills.[47] It has been suggested that Pope Innocent II was aware of these associates—or at least of mercenary sergeants-at-arms—when he referred in the early 1140s to *servientes* whom the Hospitallers were employing to ensure the safety of pilgrims,[48] although it is possible that he was thinking of the order's provision of a transportation service, centred on the *Asnerie*, its stables north of Jerusalem's walls.[49] In any case, the Hospital's militarization, like the Temple's, seems to have been born out of the religious aspirations of para-crusading or mercenary knights in Palestine.

THE CRISIS OF 1170

So mysterious is the course of events I have just described that in tracing it we are dependent on fragments of information and on archaeology. For much of the twelfth century the Hospitallers were far less communicative about their military role than were the Templars. Their near-silence masked tensions that surfaced in 1170 and took nearly a decade to resolve. They were generated by unease about the relationship between nursing the sick and warfare and by worry about resources, since the care of patients on the scale felt to be appropriate competed with a massive growth in military expenditure.

The master, Gilbert of Assailly, had made a major contribution to Christian attempts to conquer Egypt, had engaged in expensive building campaigns, and had incurred even greater costs by accepting the custody of two northern castles that had been wrecked by an earthquake and would have to be reconstructed. Evidence of his extravagance can still be seen at Belvoir, which was rebuilt soon after 1168, and in impressive works carried out at the same time at the castles of Belmont and Bethgibelin.[50] Faced by his order's near-bankruptcy and falling into what seems to have been a clinical depression, Gilbert resigned the mastership and retired to a cave to live as a hermit. In the anarchy that followed, compounded by his mood-swings, most of the brothers in Jerusalem made demands that were later confirmed by Pope Alexander III. They did not want to be weighed down by superfluous and needless expenditure, and they demanded that in future their chapter should give its consent to the acquisition of frontier castles and to any important agreements made on the order's behalf.[51]

There was, however, more to their concern than finance, and the views of the different factions among them were reflected in two papal letters of the late 1170s, which must have echoed arguments that had been transmitted to the apostolic see by the parties concerned. In *Piam admodum* Alexander reminded the Hospitallers that their first obligation was to care for the poor. They should confine their military contribution to very special occasions, which had already been defined as those on which the relic of the True Cross, usually housed in the church of the Holy Sepulchre, was carried in the Christian army, and then only if their participation was judged to be appropriate and consonant with their other obligations. The Hospital, he added, had been instituted for the reception and refection of the poor and it should concentrate on those duties, "especially as it is believed that the poor are better defended by showing them love and mercy than by force of arms."[52] At almost the same time, however, his curia reissued an earlier papal privilege, *Quam amabilis Deo*, into which passages borrowed from a letter to the Templars and describing a military function were introduced. It used to be thought that this version of *Quam amabilis Deo* was a forgery, but Rudolf Hiestand has demonstrated that it was genuine and that with these additions the curia signalled its recognition of the Hospital's military rôle.[53]

The Hospitaller leadership responded to the criticisms and to the contradictions in papal instructions by stressing that the warfare in which their order was engaged had a symbiotic relationship to the care of the sick poor. A statute, issued in 1182 and containing the first overt reference in Hospitaller legislation to a military element, must have been carefully worded, since it blandly associated fighting with acts of mercy.

> These are the special charities established in the Hospital, apart from the brothers-at-arms, which the House ought to support honourably, and many other charities which cannot be individually detailed.[54]

Another statute decreed that the order's battle standard (although it did not call it that), which was already doubling as the funeral pall of deceased brothers, was to cover the biers of poor pilgrims who had died in the hospital.[55] The concern to associate warfare with nursing may also have been expressed in a practice described by a German visitor in the 1180s, according to which the brother knights, in order to demonstrate that whatever they used belonged ultimately to the sick, had to surrender their war-horses if in the opinion of the surgeons in their field hospital there were not enough animals available to move the injured in the aftermath of battle.[56]

The dispute in the central convent had not been about the morality or otherwise of warfare, of course, but it had shown that it was not easy to persuade the members of a religious order to engage at the same time in two disparate activities, particularly when one of them departed radically from the spirit of the original foundation. It is significant that the solution found was not to abandon either of them, but to link them more closely together, ensuring that the single-minded concentration of the Templars on Christian knighthood was not going to feature in the Hospitaller ethos.

Cooperation with Church and Crown in Jerusalem

The success of the nurses in standing their ground rested on the prestige their work in Jerusalem had gained for them. Besides the main hospital there, they ran another, St Mary of the Germans,[57] in the city; a cemetery just outside;[58] an infirmary at Aqua Bella on the pilgrim road through the Judaean hills, with a shrine-church at Fons Emaus nearby;[59] a primitive ambulance service; a major almonry, particularly for nursing mothers; and a large orphanage to which a school was attached.[60] Although these multiple activities give the impression of a Byzantine or Muslim institution, as do the elaborate dietary regulations that were in place, the number of wards, and the use of resident physicians and surgeons,[61] the hospital should probably be placed in the Western tradition.[62] The norm seems to have been for its physicians to be Christian and Western-trained, although the order also allowed for the employment of those of other faiths.[63] Perhaps the best suggestion made so far is that the hospital began as and remained a western institution, but came under eastern influences as it evolved.[64]

The statutes of the 1180s and a description written at about the same time by a German priest, who had served in it, provide detailed information about the way the hospital was run.[65] The diet of the patients was lavish and they occupied separate beds, as we shall see. The ratio of staff to the infirm, which seems to have been about one to two, was generous. The hospital admitted the poor, whatever their illness (except leprosy), nationality, sex, or religion.

Further, in this holy house, which knows that the Lord, who calls
all to salvation, does not want anyone to perish, are mercifully found
men of the Pagan faith [Muslims] and Jews, if they hasten to it,
because the Lord prayed for those afflicting him, saying: *"Father,
forgive them for they know not what they do."*[66]

A respect for the dietary requirements of its Muslim and Jewish patients, who must have been pilgrims to their own shrines, may have
been reflected in a statute which laid down that the sick were to have
chicken if they could not stomach pork,[67] in references to a second
kitchen, in which the chicken was cooked,[68] and in the custom of issuing sugar, presumably to mix with water, to those who did not want
wine.[69]

The admission of non-Christians was, as far as I know, unparal-
leled in the rest of Christendom. Its origins may be found in Muslim
Jerusalem before the First Crusade. A *miraculum*, attributed to the
Hospital's founder Gerard in the mid-twelfth century, recounted how
he "had custody of the holy house and served with kindness the poor,
using alms that the Muslims gave him."[70] Presumably these alms were
the gifts of pilgrims that Muslim officials had collected on behalf of
the abbey of St Mary of the Latins. In return for them the monks may
well have been caring for non-Christians. Nevertheless, the admission
of Muslims was interpreted by at least one outsider as a solution to a
conundrum that worried thoughtful contemporaries, since it was hard
to see how a crusader could fight and at the same time express, as a
Christian must, love for his enemy. In this case, charity was being
shown to Muslim patients, any one of which could have been, or might
in future be, engaged in warfare against the very brothers who were
trying to heal him.

In this blessed house is powerfully fulfilled the heavenly teaching:
"Love your enemies and do good to those who hate you"; and elsewhere:
"Friends should be loved in God and enemies on account of God."[71]

Another function of the Hospitallers was to bury the dead. In 1143
Patriarch William of Jerusalem granted them the burial ground of

Akeldama, situated on the south side of the Hinnom Valley, which had been used for the interment of pilgrims from at least the late sixth century. It was believed to have been the Potter's Field, described in the Gospel of St Matthew as being bought for the burial of strangers by the Jewish priests with the thirty pieces of silver, the price for the betrayal of Christ, that Judas Iscariot had tried to return to them before committing suicide. The Hospitallers, who therefore became responsible for the burial not only of their patients but also of other visitors to Jerusalem, had already occupied it and had begun to build a church, dedicated to St Mary, under which there had been carved out a deep charnel pit.[72]

They were, in fact, offering a total package to those pilgrims who were unfortunate enough to fall ill. They would provide them with the best medical treatment and nursing available while they lived and would assure them of a free and decent burial should they die. In this way they were contributing to an ambitious programme, coordinated by the Church and the crown, the aim of which was to take full advantage of Jerusalem as a pilgrim centre. It was characterized by the adaptation or rebuilding in the 1140s of many of the most important shrine churches in and around the city. Much attention has been paid to the architecture and decoration of these buildings,[73] but just as impressive were the practical intentions of the planners, who seem to have wanted to make the city as "pilgrim-friendly" as possible and recognized that this involved giving thought to the visitors' peace of mind as well as to their need for prayer. Overall, the impression one has of Jerusalem in the twelfth century is of a cult-center that was being very intelligently managed.

Two slightly earlier acts of Patriarch William reinforce the impression that the Hospitallers were deeply involved in this project. In 1141 he confirmed their acquisition of Fons Emaus in the Judaean hills. This put them in possession of an important holy place because the site was believed (wrongly) to be the location of the meeting on the road between the risen Christ and two of his disciples. The order was granted full parish rights in the church, which it probably built and which still survives.[74] At about the same time William granted it another hospital, not far from the Temple, which had been recently

established for German pilgrims[75] and was the dependency out of
which, according to the Hospitallers, the Teutonic Order was to grow,
as we have seen.

The order's central role in the Church's programme for Jerusalem must have contributed to a quarrel with Fulcher of Angoulême,
William's successor as patriarch, which broke out in 1154. The osten-
sible reason for the dispute was the letter *Christiane fidei religio*, which
Pope Anastasius IV had been persuaded to issue and which, in the
course of granting the privileges the Hospital needed to become a fully
exempt order, freed it from the patriarch's ordinary jurisdiction. Its
electrifying effect has only become clear now that Rudolf Hiestand
has demonstrated that the growth of the Hospital's privileges was
far less gradual than was hitherto supposed.[76] Fulcher led a delegation
of almost the entire hierarchy of his patriarchate to Europe to appeal
against the exemption, but after a terrible journey through war-torn
Italy he was flatly turned down by Anastasius's successor, Adrian IV.
According to Archbishop William of Tyre, who was vehemently on
the side of the churchmen and devoted more space in his *Chronicle* to
this than to almost any other ecclesiastical episode, the dispute had de-
generated into violence, for which the Hospitallers were to blame, and
the pope had been bribed, but Pope Adrian was not much in favour of
exemptions and his rejection of the appeal suggests that there was less
to the patriarch's case than William made out.[77]

A second, and very revealing, reason for the quarrel was that the
Hospitallers were building a new church which William of Tyre described as being much more sumptious and higher than the church of
the Holy Sepulchre nearby.[78] It is significant that in 1150, when building work must already have begun, Queen Melisende, the patron of
much of the new architecture in Jerusalem, donated a village to this
church, on condition that after her death Mass would be celebrated annually on her behalf.[79] The construction of what must have been a truly
magnificent church—and one in which Melisende took an interest—
is a further demonstration of the close association of the Hospitallers
with the programme of city-improvement. Their rise to prominence
has often been linked to their assumption of military responsibilities,
but they could never have diversified their interests to the extent they

did without the resources that were being generated by a growing reputation for the efficiency with which they organized works of mercy, and this helps to explain why the case of the nursing faction in the order was so strong.

A Multi-Functional Order

The importance of the reconciliation of nursing with warfare, which was achieved around 1180, cannot be overestimated. It established a precedent that influenced those other orders that adopted military roles after their foundation or had the dual functions of nursing and arms-bearing, such as the Teutonic Order—although in that case the Templar ideal was going to be more prominent—and the Orders of the Swordbrothers, St Thomas of Acre and perhaps St Lazarus. Nursing remained a priority for the Hospitallers throughout the thirteenth century and the reputation of their hospital in Acre seems to have equalled that of its predecessor in Jerusalem.[80] They also continued to bury the dead. They were given permission to enclose a part of the town cemetery of Acre, which had already been designated for their use, and to build a chapel there, which was dedicated to St Michael. Visits by the faithful on the feasts of St John the Baptist, the Blessed Virgin Mary, and St Michael were indulgenced, and the chapel seems to have fulfilled the function, familiar to those who have excavated charnel chapels in Europe, of a chantry in which there was regular intercession for the dead.[81]

The Hospitallers had few infirmaries in Europe, but those westerners who had seen them at work in the East continued to acknowledge—and must have publicized—the value of their nursing of the sick. If in 1183 Duke Godfrey III of Lorraine had reported that while on pilgrimage he had witnessed the Holy Spirit at work in their humble care of the poor and the infirm in Jerusalem,[82] thirty-four years later the crusader King Andrew of Hungary was extravagant in his praise of their threefold role in Acre of caring for the sick poor, burying them, and shouldering military responsibilities,[83] and in 1268 King Louis IX of France remembered seeing with his own eyes their acts of mercy.[84]

When Eudes of Burgundy, count of Nevers, died in Acre in 1266 he bequeathed to them not his armor, but two large cooking pots from his kitchens for use in their hospital.[85]

A consequence was that even when fully developed as a Military Order the Hospital remained ambivalent about warfare. Whereas one of the seven promises the Templar brothers were supposed to make on profession was "to help conquer . . . the Holy Land and to keep and save whatever the Christians hold,"[86] the four promises made by the Hospitallers contained no reference whatever to fighting or the defence of Christendom.[87] A comparison of the Templar code with the Hospitaller statutes, *esgarts* and *usances* reveals that while 17 percent of surviving Templar legislation related to the practice of arms (105 out of 609 clauses), only 9.4 percent of Hospitaller legislation (33 out of 352) did so. The Hospitallers were, of course, intensively engaged in warfare and were judged to be effective at it. Otherwise they would never have been entrusted with major castles or shared with the Templars the most exposed positions in any Christian army's line of march.[88] And they would never have been criticized in the same terms as the Templars by commentators and crusade planners. Nevertheless, one cannot help being struck by the difference in approach manifested in their legislation. Echoes of their solution to the conflict between nursing and warfare, with its reiteration of their commitment to acts of mercy, were to reverberate throughout the centuries that followed.

Chapter Two

COMMUNITIES

RECRUITS AND REINFORCEMENTS

When he was minister of the Franciscan province in the Holy Land Fidenzio of Padua was asked by the grand master of the Temple to provide two friars to assist as chaplains at the castle of Saphet. He recalled later that when Saphet fell to the Egyptians in 1266, after nearly six weeks of siege, the garrison of two thousand defenders had been reduced to only five hundred or six hundred exhausted men, many of whom were wounded.[1] So three-quarters had perished.

At about that time there were three hundred Hospitaller brothers stationed in the East[2] and perhaps five hundred Templars. Confronting an enemy whose reserves of manpower allowed it to throw troops in headlong frontal assaults,[3] the orders could face near annihilation. They suffered terribly in the battles of the Springs of Cresson and Hattin in the summer of 1187 and in the reduction of many of their strongpoints in the months that followed: their losses at their castles of Saphet and Belvoir, which held out until early in 1189, must have been severe.[4] Even in a supposedly peaceful period, which stretched from 1200 to 1240, the Templars at Chastel Pèlerin were threatened as soon as the castle was built, and they lost one hundred out of one hundred and twenty brothers in a battle in the Amanus mountains in 1237. Hospitaller Crac des Chevaliers had to endure the attentions of the Muslims in 1207 and 1218 and Hospitaller Margat was besieged in 1206 and

1231.[5] There were regular decimations as the pace of war increased from 1240 onwards. The Templars probably sacrificed three hundred brothers and the Hospitallers two hundred in the battle of La Forbie in 1244;[6] it looks as though the orders had committed almost everyone available to the Christian army. The greater part of the Hospitaller central convent was lost in the fall of Arsur in 1265, when perhaps as many as eighty brothers were captured by the Egyptians.[7] These men faced an unpredictable prospect because at times the Muslims would order the slaughter of all prisoners belonging to a Military Order.[8]

Although the orders usually adopted a relatively dispassionate tone with respect to their foes, which was a useful counter-balance to the theatrical rhetoric of crusade preachers,[9] disasters like these generated impassioned appeals from them for help. On 16 June 1260 a Templar messenger arrived in London bringing letters for the king of England and the commander of the London Temple. He had broken all records, taking only thirteen weeks on the journey from Acre and a day to ride from Dover.[10] Among the letters he carried was one describing the Mongol invasion of Syria, addressed to all the senior Templar officials in Europe by Grand Master Thomas Berard. It detailed the conquests of the Mongols, the size and potency of their armies, the preparations made by the rulers of Aleppo and Damascus to resist them and their approaches to Egypt for an alliance, the fall of Damascus and the flight of its ruler, the speed with which the king of Cilician Armenia and the prince of Antioch-Tripoli had come to terms, the poverty of the Christians, and the order's obligations and the weight of its expenses.[11] When forty Hospitallers fell at Tripoli in 1289, Master John of Villiers demanded replacements from every western priory, in order to repopulate his convent.[12]

Appeals to the European provinces usually evoked immediate responses. Judith Bronstein has shown how experienced officers from the West, together with a new cohort of the young, were rushed out to fill the places of the Hospitallers who had died in 1187.[13] The heavy Templar casualties in the battle in the Amanus mountains in 1237 led to the mobilization in Europe of the brothers-at-arms of both orders, and thirty English Hospitallers were described riding out from their provincial headquarters in Clerkenwell, just to the north of London, on their way to the sea.[14] After the fall of Acre in 1291, in which the Templars believed that they had sacrificed three hundred brethren,[15] the brother sergeant John Senaud was present at a chapter-general in Nicosia in Cyprus attended by four hundred, nearly all of whom must have been reinforcements.[16]

New brothers could therefore be posted to the Levant immediately after their reception. Itier of Rochefort was received into the Temple at Marseilles in 1276 just as his ship was sailing.[17] Walter of Liencourt left the day after his reception in the early 1270s and remained in the Levant for twenty-four years.[18] Geoffrey of Gonneville[19] and perhaps Hugh of Faure[20] may well have departed within a matter of weeks. Hugh of Cernay and probably Bernard of Auzon left within a few months.[21] Alan Forey has suggested from an analysis of the lengths of service recorded in the fourteenth-century testimonies that a very high proportion of the Templar knights on the East were relatively new recruits.[22]

Some, perhaps many, postulants were very young. The Hospitaller knight Ferrand of Barras cannot have been more than fifteen when he was admitted in or before 1180.[23] Of the Templar knights who were active in the later thirteenth century, Hugh of Pairaud's mother had told him that he was eighteen on reception,[24] and Adam of Wallaincourt[25] and his relation Walter of Liencourt[26] cannot have been older than seventeen. These adolescents were of an appropriate canonical age in thirteenth-century terms, but Guy Dauphin had been admitted at the age of eleven,[27] and the sergeants Hugh Charnier and William of Errée had been received at twelve[28] and eight[29] respectively, although this was not unusual at a time when religious institutions were finding it difficult to divest themselves of child oblation.[30]

THE LEVANTINE COMMUNITIES

On arrival in the Levant the new brothers were allotted to communities in which they were treated as full members from the start. None of them had had the benefit of probationary training and in this respect both orders were beginning to look exceptional.[31] The Hospitallers appear never to have had a noviciate. Some Templars justified their abandonment of one by the need in time of crisis to send brothers immediately to the East, since to qualify for such service they had to be already solemnly professed.[32] A consequence was that, although learned knights were occasionally to be found,[33] most of the brothers were not well-educated, even with respect to the customs that regulated their lives.[34]

It is unlikely, therefore, that many Templars were knowledgeable enough to notice that the Office was said in a slightly different form in their new communities, since the European houses in which they had been received heard, somewhat unusually, the Office not of the order's mother church, the Holy Sepulchre, but of the dioceses in which they were situated.[35] So while both orders in Palestine observed the liturgy of the Holy Sepulchre, the Templars in the patriarchate of Antioch must have heard a different one.[36]

In other respects, however, nearly all the recruits, whether Templar or Hospitaller, must have found themselves in alien environments. After lives spent in the confines of the districts in which they had been born, surrounded by kindred they knew comparatively well, they were joining cosmopolitan communities,[37] although in the thirteenth century the Hospitallers were already refusing admission to indigenous Christians who, although presumably Uniates, were not of the Latin rite, taking the first steps towards that self-isolation that was to be a feature of their rule of their order-states until they were driven from Malta in 1798.[38] By the 1260s some effort was being made to alleviate home-sickness, because there are signs that the brothers in the Hospitaller central convent were being split into quasi-collegiate bodies, known as *langues* (tongues), that corresponded to the regions of the West from which they came,[39] and a similar process may have been at work in the Temple.[40]

The experience of the arrivals had been of commanderies which tended to be quite small. The larger ones in the West rarely housed more than twenty members and the smaller sometimes had as few as three.[41] They would therefore have found the population of their new houses daunting. The numbers in the central convents in Jerusalem and Acre fluctuated wildly, because brothers came and went and military engagements brought in those who were stationed elsewhere,[42] but William of Tyre and the Jewish traveller Benjamin of Tudela reported independently that there were as many as three hundred Templar knights in residence in Jerusalem in the 1170s.[43] These knights would have been supplemented by many brother sergeants and a few brother priests. After the loss of Jerusalem the Templar convent can rarely have been as large again, but over one hundred knights were probably living in Acre in the later thirteenth century, since that was the number described being present at a reception presided over by Grand Master William of Beaujeu.[44] This would suggest a community of perhaps two hundred brethren. Only about thirty brothers-at-arms seem to have lived in the Hospital's compound in Jerusalem in the late 1160s,[45] when the military wing was still developing, but in thirteenth-century Acre the Hospitaller convent must have consisted of well over one hundred brothers, not all of whom would have been knights, of course.

The professed comprised only a fraction of those living and working in these establishments. Hospitaller recruits must have been conscious, in ways that Templars were not, of the presence of brothers and sisters dedicated to the care of the sick. There were also large numbers of men and women, who were not conventual, working in the hospital of St John, which in Jerusalem could accommodate one thousand patients and could be enlarged in a crisis to admit as many as two thousand.[46] Each of its eleven wards was staffed by between nine and twelve servants, with more being recruited in the summer months, when fevers and water-borne diseases were common and admissions were likely to rise substantially. There were also four or five physicians and three or four surgeons, a number of bleeders and barbers, other male and female servants, including cooks and wet nurses, and many Europeans who came to do menial work as an act of devotion.[47] The total number serving the sick must have been well over five hundred, and equivalent numbers probably worked in the hospital in Acre.

Among other lay people in both headquarters, there were knights serving for pay or out of devotion,[48] senior assistants such as notaries and secretaries,[49] and many other wage-earning servants, among whom

were western and indigenous mercenaries and the technicians responsible for crossbows and artillery. And there were prisoners-of-war and
slaves. In a letter written in 1268 Master Hugh Revel of the Hospital
referred to more than ten thousand men being fed by his order in the
East.[50] A significant proportion of these must have lived in Acre, which
the orders helped garrison: Oliver of Paderborn reported that the Templars had four thousand mercenaries stationed there during the Fifth
Crusade.[51] A latrine tower, which has been discovered in the Hospitaller
compound, containing perhaps fifty stalls on two levels and associated
with a sewage pit and the town drains, must have been for the use of a
large residential population.[52] Since the convent at the Templar castle
of Saphet comprised 5 percent of the garrison, equivalent ratios would
give figures of two thousand individuals normally at work in each of
the central convents, although not all would have slept in. Even after
the fall of Acre, when the orders must have been tempted to reduce the
numbers serving in the East, there must have been at least five hundred persons at work in the Hospitaller convent in Limassol.[53]

The greater castles and commanderies also housed substantial
communities. Denys Pringle has suggested that there may have been
ten Hospitaller brothers and a total garrison of about 330 persons in
twelfth-century Belmont.[54] The establishment at Templar Saphet in
the 1260s was reckoned to be 50 brother knights, 30 brother sergeants-
at-arms, 50 turcopoles, 300 arbalesters, 820 artisans and workmen, and
400 slaves. So the convent there consisted of 80 brothers out of a garrison of 1,650, which would increase to 2,200 in time of war.[55] There
were more than twenty-four brothers in the Templar community at
Sidon in the later 1280s;[56] perhaps many more, since there were around
forty at receptions there in 1289 and 1291.[57] Thirty brothers witnessed
a reception in Tyre in the 1270s, although the grand master was pre-
siding and members of his entourage may have been present.[58] In 1255
the Hospitallers were planning to build a castle on Mt Tabor, in which
they intended to place forty knights,[59] and they envisaged garrisoning
Crac des Chevaliers with sixty,[60] although this may not have meant
a larger community than that at Saphet, since they admitted fewer
brother sergeants than did the Templars. Willbrand of Oldenburg re-

ported in 1212 that Crac's garrison numbered two thousand; he gave the other great Hospitaller castle, Margat, a peacetime complement of one thousand.[61]

Buildings

There has been very little analysis of the physical appearance of the buildings in which all these people lived and worked. There does not seem to have been a common pattern, even in Europe,[62] and many of the surviving structures in the East were anyway military, in which the needs of the religious community in residence had to be reconciled with the imperatives imposed by topography and defence. It goes without saying that defence and the need to dominate the territory around demanded a theatrical display of power, which was expressed in architecture. Many of the castles—Crac des Chevaliers, Margat, Chastel Blanc, Gaston—were the centres of lordships, which on the northern frontiers were palatinates,[63] and so had to have room for courthouses.[64] Margat also had to accommodate an episcopal curia, because the local bishop, together presumably with his chapter, lived there after 1188 and some of the canonries were in the Hospitaller master's patronage.[65]

But as they housed communities of professed religious, the construction—or in some cases adaptation—of castles and commanderies still had to be governed by the needs of the religious life. Penitential austerity was visually expressed in the simplicity that was a feature of even the most magnificent buildings and continued to be a characteristic of those constructed later by the Hospitallers on Rhodes.[66] Each community had to be provided with a chapel, a dormitory—perhaps partitioned into cells by the thirteenth century[67]—a refectory, and a chapter room, because the conventual norms were strictly enforced. It follows that enclosure—the space into which a religious community should withdraw—was an important issue, although as Anthony Luttrell has pointed out with respect to the *collachium* in the Hospitaller city of Rhodes, its purpose was not so much to keep outsiders out as to keep the brothers in.[68]

The sites of the more important commanderies, such as those in Tripoli, Antioch, Jaffa, and Tyre, have never been located, and although there are traces of the community buildings at Fons Emaus,[69] we have to rely on the greater castles for more information. Fortunately, they provide us with good examples of the need felt for enclosure.

Hospitaller Belvoir, overlooking the southern end of the Sea of Galilee, was built in a single programme shortly after 1168. There was no keep, and the form of a quadrilateral inner court was repeated in the outer walls, making this the first datable planned concentric castle. The reason for concentricity was of course military, but it was also religious, because the inner court, entered through a bent gateway, above which the chapel may have been situated, constituted the enclosure the brothers needed.[70] The form of Chastel Pèlerin, south of Haifa, built with the help of crusaders from 1217/18 onwards, was shaped by the promontory on which it stood, but it is clear from references by Oliver of Paderborn to an *oratorium* and a *palatium*, which was, he wrote, designed to be a refuge for the Templar convent from Acre, that enclosure was built into the planning from the start. This again took the form of an inner court, on one side of which there was the chapel.[71]

A few other Hospitaller and Templar castles developed organically, but with enclosure in mind. At Belmont an existing *maison-forte* (or manor house) was adapted for enclosure after an outer enceinte and an intermediate range had been constructed.[72] At Bethgibelin the original *castrum*-type fortress had outer walls added to it and a magnificent church, of the size to serve not only the Hospitaller community enclosed within but also a western burgess settlement outside, was built along one of the inner ward's external walls.[73] Chastel Blanc had a similar history to that of Belmont, but on a larger scale, with a ward encircled by outer walls. After an earthquake in 1170 had caused substantial damage, the nucleus was completely rebuilt as an *église-donjon* (tower-church), with a chapel on the lower floor.[74] The Templars may have repeated this scheme at Saphet, which also seems to have had a massive *église-donjon*.[75] The rebuilding of the castles of Crac des Chevaliers and Margat after a destructive earthquake in 1202 included spaces for enclosure, in which there were chapels. At Tortosa, enclosure spilled out from the keep to occupy a courtyard, which was bounded by a chapel and a large thirteenth-century hall.[76]

Where an order took over an existing, well-fortified locality, the inclination was to adapt rather than to rebuild. The main citadel at Sidon seems not to have been considered by the Templars for enclosure after they had bought the town in 1260. Instead they occupied the sea castle, built on a rocky islet by French and English crusaders in 1227 to 1228 and joined to the land by a causeway. They strengthened it to provide suitable accommodation for their convent, for which they constructed a chapel.[77]

The central convents combined the roles of religious houses, seats of international government, garrison barracks, and distribution centres for the orders' houses and castles scattered throughout the Levant. After the loss of Jerusalem in 1187 they were relocated to the port-city of Acre, which had been retaken by the Third Crusade, once it had been rendered habitable. The Hospitallers, keen to avoid the disturbance generated by the building of their impressive new headquarters, may not have moved there until as late as 1206. In the interim they may have established the seat of their government in their northern castle of Margat. The main argument that has been raised against this—that Margat was too far from the centre of things[78]—can be countered by pointing out that it was near the coast and was linked to Acre by sea.

The twelfth-century conventual buildings in Jerusalem are mostly lost. Some traces of Templar work in and around the al-Aqsa mosque is still visible, including a porch with three pointed arches in front of the building, a chapel, and the fragments of a cloister, but it is impossible to identify most of the structures in the vicinity.[79] The Hospitaller headquarters just to the south of the church of the Holy Sepulchre is unrecognizable, although the eleventh-century Byzantine church in which the brothers originally worshipped survives. The hospital itself, which may have been built over the many cisterns, drains, and cesspits that lie under the southern and eastern parts of the complex, close to a massive sewer which runs under David Street, must have covered most of what was a fairly constricted site.[80]

The Templars' convent in Acre, which was dominated by a fortress on the seashore, has also been almost entirely destroyed.[81] It must have shared with their castles the features of a monastic fortress, although on a larger scale. On the other hand, the sensational results of recent excavations have revealed that around 1200 the Hospitallers began an extravagant building campaign just to the north of their existing commandery. They created a large courtyard with impressive structures on the eastern and western sides and a line of huge halls along the northern boundary. The refectory could have been situated in or over a fine hall on the south side of the yard.[82] The conventual church stood immediately to the south, although only its crypt and parts of its floor have been uncovered.[83] Beyond it stood the hospital for the sick poor, which has still to be properly investigated,[84] but was not as fully integrated into the conventual buildings as had been the case in Jerusalem, probably because the order took advantage of the additional space at its disposal.

The Hospitaller compound had the appearance more of a distribution center than of a convent because important elements of the community had been transferred elsewhere. Only the master and the conventual prior, together, perhaps, with the hospitaller and the petty officers and sergeants-at-service, continued to live in the conventual buildings. The sisters, who had shared a mixed community with the brothers in Jerusalem, had been placed in their own house by 1219,[85] and the brothers-at-arms had been removed by 1230 to an *auberge*, where they lodged under the command of the marshal. Some time later they were moved again to a building in Acre's northern suburb, about 750 metres away. By the later thirteenth century this was "a very large *palais*," "very long and very beautiful," with a hall that was impressive enough to be the scene of the lavish festivities which marked a royal coronation in 1286.[86]

The order maintained, however, the fiction that all the brothers still lived on the same site. In obedience to the conventual norms the brothers-at-arms were still supposed to eat in the refectory, to which they would process from the *auberge* two by two. The marshal was responsible for seeing that they did so and that they were properly dressed.[87] And although the *auberge* had its own chapel,[88] it seems that only certain hours, such as Matins (or Vigils) in the middle of the night, were said in it. For Mass, Vespers, and probably Lauds the brothers had to come down to the conventual church, and the marshal was described standing outside with a lantern to make sure that they arrived on time.[89]

This segregation of the brothers-at-arms in Acre into a specially created enclosure was another feature that distinguished the Hospitallers from the Templars. The latter were obviously concerned about the effect on religious lives of an existence in the midst of the hurly-burly of a great administrative complex and considered relocating their convent down the coast to Chastel Pèlerin in 1218.[90] But although the grand master himself moved into his own residence in another part of Acre,[91] the convent remained where it was.

Community members

More differences become apparent when one turns to the professed religious who occupied the buildings I have described. These consisted of brother priests, knights and sergeants, and, in the case of the Hospital, sisters.

Brother priests

During the twelfth century monks and other religious were increasingly being ordained because of the need for men to say Mass and serve dependent churches, and over time the priests tended to take over the management of the communities in which they lived.[92] I have already pointed out that one of the most striking features of *Omne datum optimum*, Pope Innocent II's charter of 1139 for the Templars, was that it countered this trend. It stated that any future grand master should be "knightly and religious"[93] and, in allowing the order to have its own priests, gave it licence, as an exempt order, to dismiss those who were not suitable. Innocent added that no priest was to be introduced to chapter or promoted to the care of a community unless this was authorized by the master and brothers.[94] In the Temple, therefore, the subordinate role of priests was definitively established early on, but although an equivalent papal charter for the Hospitallers, *Christiane fidei religio* of 1154, gave them the right to have priests, who were to be subject to no one but their chapter and the papacy, there was no specific reference to them being in such a subordinate position.[95] At the time, of course, the Hospital's status as a Military Order had not yet been recognized. The pope would have considered it to be a religious institution like any other, in which any development in the role of the priests should be allowed to take its course.

In fact, Hospitaller priests, who had been serving in the order for some years before the issuing of *Christiane fidei religio*,[96] never appear to have been dominant. None of them ever held the mastership or any high office other than that of conventual prior, which was a clerical one, and the brother knights were anyway to be given precedence over them formally in the late 1230s.[97] Nevertheless the difference in approach revealed in a comparison of *Omne datum optimum* with *Christane fidei religio* suggests that the Hospital was perceived to be a more conventional religious order than was the Temple and helps to explain why in the episode in the late 1190s, which I have already described, Pope Innocent III agreed to the newly established Teutonic Order following specifically Templar practice with respect to its clergy.[98]

While Templar and Hospitaller priests could take part in chapters and magistral elections, and could also hold commanderies, at least in the West, their standing was an awkward one and the solution found to their predicament made them almost members of orders within orders. Wherever they were to be found, they answered less to the masters than to the conventual priors, the chief priests at the headquarters in Jerusalem or Acre, whose powers over them could be compared almost to those of papal vicars,[99] until, of course, any individual brother priest became himself a bishop.[100] Although the Templars do not seem to have appointed conventual priors until the thirteenth century,[101] they were often men of great influence in both orders;[102] they alone of the chief officers of the Hospital, and probably also of the Temple, were not subject to the scrutiny of chapters-general. One Templar prior, who was severely disabled, was said to have been a clever *eminence grise*, who invited the leading men of the convent to secret meetings in his room.[103]

On the other hand, the conventual priors must have been perennially anxious about the shortage of clergy at their disposal in the Levant. The Templars' need of priests was noticed by James of Vitry, who in one of his sermons to them urged them to train literate brothers, who should be sent to schools of theology.[104] Besides their duties in the convent, the hospital and the order's cemetery, Hospitaller priests had to say the *trentaine* (or thirty Masses) for every patient who died, although they could farm this out.[105] And they, and perhaps also the Templar priests, had an additional, though unofficial, cure of souls, because their churches and cemeteries were as attractive to the general public as were those of many other exempt religious orders.[106] The convent of the Templars in Acre possessed a fragment of the True Cross which was believed to have healing powers and was held by the population to be a powerful talisman in times of drought.[107] And the bishops in the Latin East, like diocesans everywhere, fought a losing battle to prevent their parishioners from attending the churches of the Hospital, receiving the sacraments from its priests, and applying for burial in its graveyards.[108]

In 1263 the Hospitaller conventual prior in Acre was responsible for seven priests, two deacons, six acolytes, and a sacristan. Although help from the two chaplains and clerk whom the master had at his personal disposal could also be enlisted, the establishment looks meager, given all the duties required of it,[109] especially if an early statute forbidding the priests to say two Masses in a day was observed.[110] There also appears to have been too few priests in dependent communities, in spite of the fact that even when they were outsiders they could enjoy the orders' privileged status.[111] A crisis of manpower in the Hospitaller commandery in Acre in 1182 must have led the master to allot the large rent of fifty besants a year to the mass-stipend of a secular priest in the commandery church.[112] Several commanderies may have become, like that in Tripoli, endowed with chantries.[113] In the early fourteenth century the Templars found it easy to refute the accusation that they had been forbidden to make confession to any but their own chaplains,[114] because their convents often sought pastoral assistance elsewhere, particularly from the Franciscans and the Carmelites. I have already referred to the grand master's request for Franciscans to be sent to Saphet.[115] The Templars in Chastel Pèlerin had a particularly close relationship with the Carmelites on Mt Carmel nearby, who received a tithe of the leftovers from the brothers' table.[116]

Brother knights and sergeants

However hard the priests had to work, most of the business of the orders was in the hands of the lay brothers, the knights and sergeants, whose role was originally modeled on that of eleventh-century *fratres conversi*, unlettered serving brothers who took the weight of administration off the shoulders of choir-monks.[117] Nearly all the high offices were reserved to knights,[118] who by the thirteenth century qualified for knighthood by being the legitimately born sons of knights.[119]

Some Templar sergeants in France were the kin of brother knights[120] and one sergeant claimed to be noble, although it is not clear why he had never been knighted,[121] but most, like the Englishman Ralph, who had been a mercer before entering the order,[122] must have come from merchant, artisan or richer peasant stock because on the one hand their fathers were not knights and on the other they had to promise at profession that they were not of servile status. In both orders they were categorized as those -at-arms and those -at-service, but they made up a much larger and more important component of the Temple than was the case in the Hospital. Figures for the French-speaking territories in Europe collected by Damien Carraz are very striking. Provence, where there were twice as many Templar sergeants as knights, was in his opinion markedly more "aristocratic" than Auvergne, where the sergeants outnumbered the knights by five to one, and Paris, where the sergeants outnumbered the knights by eight to one.[123]

Templar sergeants spanned a very wide range of education[124] and skills, in France from the treasurer of the Paris Temple, who was in effect the banker to the French crown, to shepherds and laborers. Many French sergeants-at-service were engaged in the kind of menial work that in the Hospital was the responsibility of servants. The same range of expertise was to be found among the Templars in the Latin East, where the sergeants must also have constituted a majority of the

brothers, although probably a smaller one than in the West and perhaps concentrated at the central convent and in the greater commanderies. Many of them occupied petty administrative positions,[125] but
they are also to be found as treasurers or chamberlains in Acre and
Tripoli.[126] At the other end of the scale there are references to a mason
in Acre,[127] a blacksmith and a cobbler at Saphet,[128] and a shepherd at
Chastel Blanc.[129]

The greater use made of paid servants by the Hospital meant that
there were fewer Hospitaller sergeants in the East, whether -at-arms
or -at-service—indeed, only the master had the right to receive a man
into the order as a sergeant-at-arms[130]—and no evidence for any in
menial occupations. Most held the same kinds of minor office as did
their Templar counterparts.[131] Few reached the heights of the better
educated Templar sergeants, although they always seem to have been
appointed to the infirmary for sick brothers[132] and could be found serving in the treasury in Jerusalem.[133]

The status of knights relative to sergeants was several degrees
higher in the Temple than it was in the Hospital. Government of the
latter was, of course, firmly in the knights' hands, but all Hospitaller
sergeants seem to have ranked as "conventuals" and so could attend
chapter, whereas many, if not most, of those in the Temple belonged to
an underclass that had no voice in order business.[134] Templar knights
wore white. A fresco painted in a Templar church in Italy in the 1260s
appears to depict them in cowled habits looking not unlike Cistercian
monks,[135] but if the painter really intended to portray the Templars
he knew, these brothers may have been wearing a regional variation
in dress, because it seems to have been more usual for them to wear
mantles. At any rate, the knights' white clothing sharply distinguished
them from brother priests and sergeants, who wore brown.[136] The
only other brothers entitled to wear white were those priests who became bishops.[137] So obsessed with this issue did the Templars become
that they challenged the right of the Teutonic Knights to wear mantles
similar to their own.[138]

In the Hospital, on the other hand, a distinction in battle dress between knights and sergeants-at-arms, which was introduced as late as

1259—the knights were to wear a red surcoat with a divisional white cross on it—was abolished nineteen years later.[139] This may have been because of a more relaxed attitude towards uniformity of dress. Although black always seems to have been the norm for peacetime conventual wear, probably because the Hospital had originated in an off-shoot of the Cassinese Benedictine abbey of St Mary of the Latins, it was not specified in the Rule as compulsory.[140] Only in 1305, when an effort was made at standardization, was it definitively established as the color of the conventual habit.[141]

The enhanced status of the Templar knights probably derived from the order's single-minded commitment to warfare, but it may also have been a caste reaction to the large number of sergeants in the order. The knights were normally deferred to. At multiple receptions they received their mantles first. Sergeants do not seem to have been entitled to receive knights and there survives a description of a sergeant-commander, who was a receptor, asking a knight who was present to give a postulant his mantle.[142] Although sergeants could be appointed to senior posts in Europe and could have relatively easy relationships with knights,[143] there is evidence that steps were taken to keep them in their place. The experienced sergeant John Senaud, who had served in Palestine and Cyprus and had been the commander of two important houses in France, reported to one of the early fourteenth-century commissions of inquiry that Peter of Madic, the grand commander of Auvergne and Limoges, had expressed contempt for sergeants, saying that they should always behave as though they were "deaf, dumb and blind."[144]

Sisters

The Hospital was also distinguished from the Temple in having a substantial body of nuns, comprising by 1338 almost 30 percent of the known professed members of the order resident in England and Wales.[145] Although some women travelled to the East,[146] it must have been more usual for them to enter Hospitaller nunneries in western Europe, where in most cases they joined enclosed communities simi-

lar to those of canonesses regular, because in the last third of the twelfth
century, in a fashion typical of the time, the order was segregating
the sisters into single-sex houses, each of which was administered by a
prioress, subject in Europe to the Hospitaller provincial. She attended
the annual provincial chapter and sent to the provincial headquarters
the equivalent of responsions.[147]

Sisters had lived alongside the brothers in the twelfth-century
convent in Jerusalem. These "matrons of advanced years, of widow-
like continence," had been responsible for the orphanage, but they had
also worked in the kitchens and may have had some sort of supervisory
role in the women's wards.[148] A separate nunnery had been established
for them in Acre by 1219,[149] but no details survive of their life there
or of the role of its prioress within the order. Most of the sisters must
have been recruited locally, and in a bid to expand its female establishment the Hospital persuaded the pope in 1256 to grant it the famous
nunnery of St Lazarus of Bethany, now in exile in Acre. It intended
to introduce its own sisters gradually as the nuns of St Lazarus died
out, but the next pope, who as patriarch of Jerusalem had opposed the
grant in the first place, quashed it in 1261.[150] The prospect of swal-
lowing St Lazarus must have inspired a statute that relaxed the condi-
tions for admitting women from the local population, "considering the
profit . . . that could come to the house if they should receive the sisters
and the losses . . . if they should refuse to receive them."[151]

In the context of religious life in general the flourishing female
component in the Hospital was conventional. Benedictines, including
Cluniacs and Cistercians, Camoldensians, Grandmontines, Carthusians,
Premonstratensians (for a time), Dominicans, and Franciscans generated female houses. It was in the context of the Military Orders that
nuns were unusual; only the Iberian order of Calatrava had sisters of a
similar sort.[152] Although a few independently minded women attached
themselves to the Temple and there was a short-lived female commandery in Aragon, established through the influence of a rich patroness
who became its *commendatrix*,[153] the Templars never formally recognized a female membership and may well have discouraged women
from joining them. But the histories of other religious orders show

that discouragement rarely put women off if they were determined to adopt a particular form of life. The Temple cannot have attracted them. The Hospital did, perhaps because of its role as a dispenser of mercy.

— It is hard to exaggerate the importance of the care of the sick in shaping the character of the Hospital and in distinguishing it from the Temple. It was, of course, a Military Order governed by lay brothers, but in its approach to enclosure, its nuns, its treatment of sergeants and greater use of servants it conformed more closely than did the Temple to the norms of the religious life.

Chapter Three

GOVERNANCE

In a letter written in 1260 Grand Master Thomas Berard of the Temple exclaimed: "there is not a prince in this world who could conveniently hold seven castles at the same time . . . and add [to this] the costs involved in the defence of such a great city as Acre, a major part of which falls on us."[1] Eight years later his opposite number in the Hospital, Hugh Revel, made much the same point when he was stressing his order's desperate need of funding.[2] Drawing on resources from Europe in a way denied to many of the institutions in the Latin East, the orders were better placed than others to make up for losses in attritional warfare, but there was a limit to what they could do, and the strain often showed.

The Templars had lost many of their castles in the kingdom of Jerusalem in the aftermath of the battle of Hattin,[3] but for a few years after 1229 they may have moved back into Chastel Hernault, at the entrance to a corridor linking Jerusalem to the coast,[4] and by the time Thomas Berard was writing they had acquired Chastel Pèlerin[5] and had reoccupied Saphet.[6] They were soon to buy the city and lordship of Sidon and the castle of Beaufort in a deal financed by a special levy raised on their European houses.[7] In the county of Tripoli they had held on to the fortresses of Chastel Blanc,[8] Aryma[9] and Tortosa,[10] and in the principality of Antioch they had reestablished their convent-garrisons—Gaston,[11] Trapessac,[12] Port Bonnel,[13] Roche Roussel[14] and Roche Guillaume[15]—along the line of the Amanus mountain chain, which closed Syria from Cilicia.[16] Gaston, astride the pass known as the Syrian Gates, was the most important of these until it was abandoned, together with Port Bonnel and Roche Roussel, in the wake of the fall of the city of Antioch in 1268,[17] but the order maintained a garrison in Roche Guillaume and a presence in the neighbouring port of Calamella until 1298.[18]

The Hospitallers had hung on to Crac des Chevaliers in the county of Tripoli[19] and Margat in the principality of Antioch.[20] They had been established for a time at Camardesium above Seleucia in the kingdom of Cilician Armenia.[21] But they had never recovered their southern castles of Bethgibelin,[22] Belmont,[23] and Belvoir,[24] although these, like Saphet, were in districts ceded back to the Christians in 1229 and in 1241. Perhaps they could not afford to reoccupy them.

Warfare in an age of rapid technological development was very costly, quite apart from the time and effort needed when building large, and especially concentric, castles. The Templars were still at work on Vadum Jacob, the construction of which had been begun by the king of Jerusalem in October 1178, when it fell to Saladin in August 1179.[25] When Saphet was rebuilt in the mid thirteenth century the cost was estimated by the Templars to be 1,100,000 saracen besants.[26] Since mercenary knights were serving in Palestine for 120 besants a year,[27] this was the equivalent of paying a year's wages to over 9,000 knights.

Castles needed garrisons, and the cost of mercenaries was a very heavy charge. In 1275 the troops the new grand master of the Temple, William of Beaujeu, had brought with him from Europe rioted in Acre and threatened to go over to the Muslims if their wages were not settled.[28] In addition, there were the expenses of upkeep and provisioning. In 1212 the traveller Willbrand of Oldenburg reported that the policy at Margat was to store five years' worth of provisions for its garrison of 1,000 men.[29] The annual bill for the maintenance of Saphet came to 40,000 saracen besants,[30] the equivalent of bearing a permanent establishment of 333 knights. Resupplying arrangements broke down badly in 1268, when Gaston had to be abandoned by the Templars because it was short of men and provisions.[31]

The Hospitallers were uncomfortable with the fact that their military role in the south was now confined to occupying two estate fortlets[32] and helping to defend Acre. They announced their intention to fortify and garrison Mt Tabor in 1256[33] and they took over what turned out to be the last-ditch defences of Ascalon between 1243 and 1247[34] and Arsur between 1261 and 1265.[35] These commitments must have saddled them with huge bills, but one is still left with the impression that they did not have the war-resources in Palestine to match the Templars.

It was not that the Hospitallers were poorer. A well-informed contemporary believed that they had twice as much property in Europe as had the Templars.[36] He may have been wrong, but it is hard in the light of his remark to suppose that the Hospitallers were less well endowed. It is more likely that their hospitals,[37] orphanages, and almonries drained away their resources. The demands these made on them become clear when one considers what was entailed in the provision of nursing care at their main hospital in Jerusalem, which was replicated in Acre after 1200.

Up to a thousand patients occupied properly constructed beds—in an age when such beds were rare—and the babies in an obstetrical ward had little cots so that they would not be disturbed by their mothers. The beds had linen sheets, feather mattresses, and coverlets, which were changed every fortnight; and rugs and furs were provided in winter.

Every week the brothers in charge of the wards purchased a wide selection of fruit and vegetables—including pomegranates, apples, pears, plums, figs, dried figs, grapes, chestnuts, almonds, dried lettuce, chickory, radishes, purslain, rock-parsley, parsley, cucumbers, lemons, gourds, and melons—for the patients, who generally had a salad served with their supper on two days a week. There are references to "normal portions" of fruit being served every day and to additional amounts of it on Fridays. In an age when very few people ever had white bread or large quantities of meat, every patient got half a loaf of white bread a day, supplemented by the coarse loaves baked for the community. Pork, mutton, or goat, or, if the sick could not stomach these, chicken "in a good sauce, well-seasoned and cooked with saffron," were served on three days a week. The Hospitallers specified that the meat should be butchered in generous portions from goats and lambs not yet one year old and sheep and pigs that were only one year old. Doves and partridges were also provided. On the other days of the week corn cakes were served, together with chickpeas and almonds on Fridays and four boiled eggs on Wednesdays and Saturdays.[38] Broth and cooked dishes of vegetables and barley flour, and "other foods suitable for the sick," were to be given to them on the advice of a doctor. On certain days double rations were issued; "and for the frail should be prepared whatever they ask for."

The season of fasting in Lent had relatively little effect on the dietary regime, probably because it was felt that it was important to keep the patients well nourished. So Lent opened with a meal of leeks and fresh pork, with chicken in the evening. During the rest of the season, the patients had fresh fish three times a week (or salted fish if fresh could not be found), often issued to them in double rations. On the other four days they were fed on almonds or rice with chickpeas and raisins or other fruit. On Good Friday, however, all fasted on bread and water, although the patients were also given wine.[39] When one considers that the Templar garrison of 1,650 men at Saphet had to be supplied with 12,000 mule loads of grain each year,[40] the demands on the Hospitallers, who had to provide so much food, furniture, and bedding, and convey it to Jerusalem and later to Acre, is almost beyond imagination.

To meet the bills the orders relied greatly, of course, on the responsions in cash and kind rendered from their European estates and from the relatively secure island of Cyprus.[41] But the transportation of resources across the Mediterranean was subject to many variables and was never reliable, and they had to pay attention to potential sources of funds nearer home. In the twelfth century they must have profited from their custody of shrines in Palestine and Syria, although these had to be provided with vestments, church furniture, communion vessels, and reliquaries, and the interiors of the churches had to be decorated.[42] The shrines had not been of the first importance, although had they been located in Europe each would have been a major cult center. But in the thirteenth century the Templars were no longer living in their buildings on the edge of the Temple esplanade;[43] and the Hospitallers had lost their headquarters in Jerusalem, which they had persuaded the pope to identify with a hospice founded by the Maccabees, ruled by Zachary, the father of St John the Baptist, and frequented by Christ,[44] together with their stational church and cemetery at Akeldama[45] and their church at Fons Emaus, which, as has already been mentioned, was one of two sites competing for the location of Emmaus of the New Testament.[46] In the thirteenth century the Templars were left with an interest in the shrine of St George of Somelaria, north of Acre,[47] and perhaps in the church reputed to be the first one dedicated to the Blessed Virgin Mary, which had been incorporated into the cathedral of Tortosa,[48] while pilgrims who visited the headquarters of both orders in Acre could gain indulgences.[49] The contribution these made to revenue cannot have been very significant.

It is therefore understandable that they were always trying to maximize the income generated by their real estate on the Levantine mainland. They owned a few towns[50] and many villages, most of which had been given to them in alms and so were exempted from the jurisdiction of secular courts,[51] urban houses and shops, and suburban vineyards and gardens, together with revenue-bearing assets such as ovens,[52] bath-houses,[53] soapworks,[54] glassworks,[55] fisheries,[56] and mills.[57] The communities of brothers responsible for the management of these properties were lodged either in their castles, which, unless they dominated their neighbourhoods like Chastel Pèlerin or Margat, were themselves a drain on funds,[58] or in their commanderies, the greatest of which were in the chief towns of the settlements: Tyre,[59] Tripoli,[60] and Antioch.[61] The Templar land commanders of Tripoli, Antioch, and Cyprus, whose houses must have mirrored the central convent as distribution centers, had establishments that were similar to those in Acre,[62] as did the greater castellans and commanders: Templar at Gaston,[63] Chastel Blanc,[64] Tortosa,[65] Sidon,[66] Saphet,[67] and Chastel Pèlerin;[68] and Hospitaller at Crac des Chevaliers,[69] Margat,[70] and probably Tripoli and Antioch.

Some of the initiatives the orders took illustrate how keen they were for cash. Their sugarcane plantations, situated on well-watered lands by the coast, and the sugar factories associated with them, were highly profitable, although they needed substantial investment in irrigation channels, refineries, and mills.[71] Hundreds of sugar pots were recently discovered in one of the halls of the Hospitaller convent in Acre, carefully stacked in preparation for distribution to the plantations in the following season.[72] Some Hospitaller villages must have been converted to the cultivation of sugarcane, because the bishop of Acre demanded a reestimation of their tithes.[73] The change cannot have been welcomed by the peasants, who would now be required to perform labor services that seem to have taken up the whole of October,[74] but Judith Bronstein has suggested that the returns from the plantations helped the Hospital to meet the expenses entailed in the reconstruction of its castles of Crac des Chevaliers and Margat after the earthquake of 1202 without an overreliance on its European estates.[75]

The orders followed other landlords in establishing colonial settlements for European immigrants,[76] but most of their villages were inhabited by indigenous peasants who were accustomed to a system of agriculture in which there was no demesne land (or home farm) to speak of and to landlords who were on the whole absentee and content to take their customary shares of the harvest. It was in everybody's interest to disturb these traditional practices as little as possible, but I have already referred to the imposition of labor services on villages turned over to sugar production, and there are signs that the Hospitallers forced equally radical changes on others in order to provide for their patients. In the 1180s six villages near Jerusalem, only one of which appears to have been a western colonial settlement, were made to specialize "in fruits, bucks, ewes, goats, pigs and hens"; two were also given over to the production of wheat.[77] One of these must have been subjected very quickly to alteration for it to feature in a statute issued only a year or two after its purchase.[78] In the thirteenth century a village near Acre was dedicated to poultry[79] and two to wheat and barley.[80] The brothers must again have had the difficult task of persuading the peasants to change their methods of cultivation.

GOVERNMENT

New arrivals in the East could not fail to have noticed the scale and variety of the orders' activities, the international dimension of their obligations, and the consequential hierarchy of officers, each with his own department. After an experimental period that lasted for most of the twelfth century, the headquarters staff in both orders took the forms they were to maintain until 1291.[81]

Masters and convents

The masters of the Temple and the Hospital were elected by a special chapter consisting of the brothers serving in the Levant, although in the Temple and probably, given the emergence of the *langues*, in the Hospital as well, an effort was made to ensure that the electors were of different nationalities. Any representation from overseas would have been impractical, given the time it took to cross the Mediterranean, and it was inevitable that most masters came from the ranks of those already in the East.[82] Indeed, of the twenty-three grand masters and twenty-four masters who ruled the Temple and the Hospital respectively from 1120 to 1307, only seven in each order are known to have been translated from the West.[83]

Although in both orders a class of conventual brothers known as *prudhommes* may have functioned collectively as advisers,[84] there is no evidence for a magistral council in the Hospital until after our period and a solitary reference—with respect to the rebuilding of Saphet[85]—to one in the Temple. The Templar or Hospitaller master together with his convent constituted the executive body. The consent of the convents was essential to admissions, to transfers to other orders, and to a wide range of agreements, including those on property, and even the Templar grand masters were supposed to be bound by them.[86]

But the grand masters had greater powers, reminiscent of those enjoyed by Benedictine abbots in earlier centuries, than their counterparts in the Hospital, who found themselves engaged every now and then in a constitutional tug-of-war with their convents and chapters-general.[87] The rule of William of Beaujeu from 1273 to 1291 illustrates how autocratic a Templar master could be. William, whose family was related by marriage to the kings of France,[88] ruthlessly paved the way for the controversial assumption by Charles of Anjou of the crown of Jerusalem and then took on the role of Charles's agent in Acre.[89] He personally initiated a close relationship with the Egyptian Mamluks and his secretary, who knew Arabic, recorded the friendship he had with an amir called Salah, who in return for valuable gifts was accustomed to let him know when a Mamluk advance was planned and sent warning of Sultan Qala'un's intention to take Acre.[90] Many in the order were not happy about this, and it is an indication of the general mood that one of William's supporters, Matthew Sauvage, the commander of Sidon, was rumoured to have been a blood brother of the Mamluk sultan Baybars.[91] James of Molay recalled three decades later the discontent he and many of the pugnacious young brothers serving in Acre in the 1270s and 1280s had felt with what they considered to be appeasement. James added that eventually they came to terms with William's policy.[92] There was, in fact, little they could have done about it, but a sense of frustration may have contributed to the low-level tension that seems to have been a feature of life in the Templar convent. Hugh of Faure, who had served in the east for fourteen years, had never witnessed the reception of a postulant in Acre, because, he told the papal commissioners in Paris, it was hard to get the brothers there to agree on the suitability of any candidate; instead, aspirants had to be sent to other Levantine communities, where agreement was more achievable because there were fewer brothers in residence.[93]

Chapters-general

The authority of the Templar grand masters was symptomatic of their order's commitment to warfare. Armies do not function well if managed by committees. But a consequence was an increasingly archaic constitution, characterized by weak systems of control and representation. The term chapter-general had originally been used throughout the Church to refer to a meeting of all the choir monks residing in a Benedictine abbey and those dependent priories that were nearby, but a feature of regular life in the twelfth and thirteenth centuries had been the emergence of new forms, attended by the representatives of distant houses or provinces. Much of the business of these chapters was similar to that undertaken by lower ones in local communities or at provincial level, but to their other functions was often added the exceptionally important one of legislation, which could take the form of statutes.[94]

Templar chapters-general in the East decided major disciplinary cases and gave final approval for the transfer of brothers back to Europe and for the grand master's appointments to the great offices.[95] They would strongly uphold what they perceived to be their rights, even against the papacy. The failure of a raid into the Palestinian hinterland in 1260 was blamed on the behavior of the marshal Stephen of Cissey, who was said to have squabbled over some woman with the order's ally, the lord of Beirut. He lost his habit and was sent to Europe. His habit was soon restored to him, but when Pope Urban IV, who as a former patriarch of Jerusalem was familiar with the case, intervened to remove him from office, the order enraged the papacy by sending him back to Rome bearing the message that it was not for a pope to interfere in this way.[96]

Templar chapters-general had two particular features, however. First, they had no independent authority. The grand master and his convent were considered to comprise the sole legislature, with prerogative rights that were affirmed over and over again in the brothers' responses to their interrogators in the early fourteenth century. It followed that the chapters-general were legislatures only because the grand master and his convent were present at them, and that their statutes were not binding unless the master and his convent had agreed to them.[97] This may be why the statutes do not appear to have been circulated and survive only in summary form. It is indicative of the balance of power in the order that the grand master and his convent sent copies of their decisions, rather than those of chapters-general, to their representatives in the west, the masters *deça mer* and later the visitors-general, who were supposed to transmit them through the provincials to the brothers at large.[98]

Secondly, there is no evidence that western grand commanders came as a matter of course to the chapters-general in the East, which were attended by the commanders of the great bailiwicks and the more important castellans in the Levant.[99] It has been suggested that, given their four-year terms of service, the retirements of some European grand commanders could statistically have coincided with meetings in which they could have taken part, provided the chapters met every four or five years,[100] or alternatively that the chapters were convened annually, which would have ensured the presence of at least some retiring western provincials.[101] But the only evidence for annual meetings is a clause in an agreement, drawn up between the Templars, the Hospitallers, and the Teutonic Knights in 1258, which stated that it should be recited each year in their chapters-general.[102] This may have been the expression of a pious wish, because there is no other sign that it was usual practice for Templar chapters-general, or Hospitaller ones for that matter, to meet regularly, let alone annually. And if the western provincials were consistently absent—and no allowance seems to have been made for their presence—these chapters cannot have been representative of the Temple as a whole.

Hospitaller chapters-general had more power and seem to have been correspondingly more effective. One in 1206[103] underlined the gulf opening up with the Temple when it stated that a Hospitaller master did not have to be present for statutes to be valid; this was all the more striking because much of its legislation showed signs of Templar influence.[104] It also imposed significant limitations on magistral authority when it defined the oath a master should take. And although the master could convoke and preside over a chapter-general, he was bound to take advice at every stage. Whereas his counterpart in the Temple appointed the great officers himself with the consent of chapter,[105] the Hospitaller master had no vote in their election, although he chose the committee and its president and was to be consulted by it, while the *ex officio* participation of his companions—two brother knights who were his personal advisers—gave him an indirect voice in the proceedings. It is true that in the course of the thirteenth century the masters were able to recover some of the ground they had lost, and that statutory legislation in defiance of their wishes would have been usually unthinkable, but the serious way in which Hospitaller statutes were treated is underlined by their diffusion throughout Europe,[106] which suggests that they were circulated to the provinces.

Hospitaller chapters-general, moreover, developed into representative legislatures.[107] If early in its history the Hospital had been ruled, as the Temple always was, directly by the master and his convent,[108] the constitutional crisis of the late 1160s had brought provincial officers to Jerusalem from overseas, since the priors of Apulia and Messina were staying there.[109] Regular European representation seems to have been introduced in the 1180s, after which the priors serving in Europe were supposed to come to a chapter-general to render account of their performance, although most of them may well have found themselves unable to do so.[110] In their legislative activity and in the development of representation Hospitaller chapters-general corresponded to what was becoming the norm in Latin religious life. In other words, the constitution of the Hospital progressed in line with developments elsewhere in the Church, whereas the constitution of the Temple remained locked in the form it had assumed by the middle of the twelfth century.

Capitular bailiffs

In the late thirteenth century William of Santo Stefano, a Hospitaller knight and the first serious historian of his order, compared the role of the master of the Hospital to that of a sea captain, who ran a ship but did not himself climb the rigging or set the sails. A master, William maintained, should not interfere with the day-to-day management of the central offices, each of which was headed in both orders by a capitular bailiff.[111] By the thirteenth century some of the great officers in the Temple and the Hospital had similar titles: marshal (the military chief), grand commander (responsible for general administration and provisioning), drapier (in charge of stores, tailoring, bedclothes and the like), conventual prior (head of the ecclesiastical establishment), and turcopolier (in command of the mercenaries). Others were to be found only in one order: hospitaller in the Hospital, and in the Temple the commander of the knights of the convent, who was technically subject to the grand commander and the marshal but seems to have had such important duties that he ranked with the seniors.[112] It is, incidentally, indicative of the Hospital's less single-minded commitment to military affairs that its post of commander of knights was ad hoc, being filled only when an expedition was launched into Islamic territory or when someone had to be left in charge at the convent when the rest of the brothers had gone beyond the frontiers of the kingdom of Jerusalem.[113]

The author of the most exhaustive study of these posts has concluded that the offices of grand commander and marshal were usually held by brothers who had already had experience of relatively high office in the Levant or in Europe; that military experience seems not unreasonably to have come into the picture when an individual was assessed for the marshalcy; that individuals continued to be appointed to senior positions after completing terms as grand commander or marshal; that the office of drapier was not given to very senior brothers but was a stepping stone to advancement; and that, at least in the Hospital, the need for reliable treasurers meant that successful ones tended to be reappointed, with Joseph Chauncy's twenty-three years in post being a striking example.[114]

It is not surprising to find that among the great officers of the Temple there was no hospitaller and that the marshal was second-in-command to the grand master. In the Hospital, on the other hand, the marshal, although in charge of all the brothers-at-arms and the leader of the convent as a body, ranked after the grand commander, whose higher status was probably due to the authority he had throughout the Latin East, whereas the Templar grand commander shared responsibilities with opposite numbers—themselves also known as grand commanders—in Tripoli, Antioch, and Cyprus.[115]

This division by the Templars of the region into four provinces needs explanation, given that in Europe they had a penchant for much larger units of provincial government than had the Hospitallers.[116] It may have reflected the fact that, with more brothers and a greater number of important castles, they had more communities to manage. Or it may have been that they had opted for the structure that best suited the geography of the region—the Hospitaller bailiffs in

Tripoli, Antioch, Armenia, and Cyprus certainly had a degree of financial independence[117]—and that it was the needs of the hospital at the
headquarters that had forced the Hospitallers to centralize their management of the Levant to ensure a steady flow of supplies.

CAREER DEVELOPMENT

Although many sergeants-at-service, like the Templars Dominic
of Dijon, who was a farm labourer, and Helias Costati from Saintes,
who was "simple" and had care of his commandery mills, must have
lived out their lives in the European houses,[118] a normal starting point
in both orders for the careers of knights and sergeants-at-arms was
service in the Levant,[119] just as it may have been common, at least until
Palestine became too dangerous, for elderly Templars to retire to the
central convent at the end of their careers.[120] I have already described
how young many of the arrivals in Palestine could be. At some point
a decision would have had to be made about each individual's aptitude
for life in the East and the type of activity that suited him. For example,
the brothers in the Hospital who reached the very senior post of hospitaller may have been directed from early on into a career in nursing,
because of the fifteen known holders of that bailiwick before 1291 only
two are recorded occupying any other office. Craph became lieutenant
master and Peter of Hagham prior of England.[121] Neither post required
special expertise, although both would have demanded exceptional
administrative ability.[122] It has been suggested that the office of hospitaller was in career terms a "dead end" one,[123] but it is surely better to
view it as the summit of a life dedicated to nursing. At any rate, the details of the careers of many brother knights may be lost to us because
of their commitment to less high-profile work among the sick.

The question may also have been asked whether the potential a
young man demonstrated made him more suitable for managerial life
in the West. A number of brothers may have spent their lives entirely,
or mostly, in the East, but some seem to have had a comparatively short
spell there initially.[124] Once back in Europe, several of them were not
destined to stay for very long, because in time they would be ordered

back across the Mediterranean. Adhémar of Peyrousse, for example, was commander of Le Bastit in southern France in the 1260s before becoming castellan of Tortosa and commander of Sidon.[125] It was also possible, however, to build a successful career at home. Four Hospitaller priors of St Gilles had risen through holding western commanderies.[126] William of Sonnac was elected to the grand mastership of the Temple in 1247 after a long sojourn in the West, although this may have been in anticipation of the crusade of King Louis IX of France, which would reach the East in the following year.[127] Hugh of Pairaud, who was received into the Temple in 1262, seems to have spent almost all his life in Europe, holding a succession of commanderies before becoming grand commander of France and visitor-general. On the strength of this *curriculum vitae* he was a serious contender for the mastership in 1292.[128]

Senior brothers in both orders found themselves being switched to and fro across the Mediterranean to higher offices in both East and West. An extraordinary example was Ferrand of Barras, if indeed we are dealing with one man, rather than with an uncle and a nephew. A brother in 1180 in the priory of St Gilles, Ferrand had come to the Levant by 1194, presumably in the cohort of replacements for the losses in 1187. By 1214 he had been made castellan of the important new castle of Camardesium in Cilicia. After commanding a force sent to Antioch in 1219 he was made marshal of the order during the Fifth Crusade. He had been replaced by 1232 and in 1246 he was sent back to his homeland as prior of St Gilles. In 1259, by which year he was presumably aged ninety-four, responsibility for a group of western provinces was attached to his priory.[129]

FAMILY OR SOCIAL INFLUENCE

One of the reasons for seeking—or being pushed into—profession in the Temple, and probably in the Hospital, seems to have been a family tradition of order-membership.[130] Long-standing relationships, built up over generations, with commanderies in the European countryside[131] led to the concentration of vocations in certain kin-groups. Roger of Bort, who was a brother knight and must have been a widower, was present when his son Renard of Bort was received into the Templar commandery of Bellechassagne by his brother Franco of Bort, grand commander of Limoges and Aquitaine.[132] Hugh of Pairaud, who had been received into the Temple by his uncle, Humbert of Pairaud, grand commander of France and visitor-general, was himself the uncle of the knight commander Hugh of Chalon-sur-Saône.[133] Raimbaud of Caromb, the Templar grand commander in Cyprus in the early fourteenth century, was probably the nephew of his namesake, who had been grand commander of Provence.[134] Adam of Wallaincourt and his brother were related to Walter of Liencourt.[135] Although toponyms can be very misleading, it looks as though many families provided more than one sergeant to the Temple. In the early fourteenth century the Charniers from Auvergne, who included William Charnier, the grand commander of Rome with the highest rank known to me reached by any sergeant, seem to have had five members in the order simultaneously.[136] The Grandevilles had five, probably six,[137] and the St Justs three, probably four.[138]

The Hospitallers were never subjected to the quizzing endured by the last generation of Templars, and their family relationships are therefore harder to establish. William of Villiers, who was grand commander in 1192 and was sent to the West in the following year as grand commander of *Outremer* and became prior of England by 1199 and prior of France by 1207, may have been a great or great-great uncle of the master John of Villiers.[139] William of Montaigu, drapier in 1233, may have been related to the master Garin of Montaigu.[140] A namesake of the master Peter of Vieille Bride was turcopolier in Acre a few years after Master Peter's death and may have been his nephew.[141] Thomas Lorne, a magistral companion, may have been related to the later master, Nicholas Lorgne.[142] William of Villaret, elected master in 1296, was succeeded in 1305 by his nephew Fulk, whose career had benefited greatly from this relationship.[143] Joscelin of Tournel, marshal in 1262, was probably the uncle of another Joscelin, who was grand commander in 1306.[144]

Given the family traditions of commitment, nepotism should not be assumed as a matter of course, although cases of it must have occurred. Nor should undue favoritism be necessarily imputed to those masters who judged some of their subordinates worthy of high office. The Hospitaller master William of Châteauneuf seems to have identified Hugh Revel as someone of real ability. Hugh succeeded him as master and in his turn helped on the career of his successor Nicholas Lorgne. The Templar master Thibault Gaudini had owed advancement to his two predecessors, Thomas Berard and William of Beaujeu.[145]

Social status seems to have been more important than mere kinship, at least in the Temple. For some decades of the twelfth century the Temple pursued what proved to be the unwise policy of recruiting high ranking lay settlers—Philip of Nablus (or Milly), Eudes of St Amand, and Gerard of Ridefort—and rapidly promoting them to the mastership. Several leading figures in the order came from well-known European families, some with a long tradition of crusading behind them. Among the leading Templars in the thirteenth century, Humbert and Hugh of Pairaud were nobles from Forez,[146] and Amaury of la Roche, grand commander in Acre and then grand commander of France, may have been born into a branch of the family of the counts of Namur.[147] The twelfth-century grand masters, Robert Burgundio and Robert of Sablé, were the descendants of a first crusader and came from a circle of castellan families in the district immediately to the north of Angers, which was a centre of crusading enthusiasm from early on.[148] Grand Master William of Beaujeu was descended from the Montlhéry family, the clan most committed to early crusading, and every one of his direct ancestors since 1146 had taken the cross. Three of his brothers were in the army of Louis IX of France that descended on Tunis in 1270, and one died there; the eldest perished on the Aragonese crusade of 1285.[149] Bertrand, Geoffrey, Hugh, and Roncelin of Fos came from a Provençal family with relations in the county of Tripoli.[150]

It is not easy to identify the origins of most Hospitaller brothers. It is clear that commanders in the West usually came from the neighborhood of their houses, as did provincial priors,[151] but it is hard to locate them and their families precisely. One has the impression that although all brother knights came from the class of arms-bearers, the Templars tended to attract individuals of a slightly higher social status than did the Hospitallers. Of the twenty-three Templar and twenty-four Hospitaller masters reigning in the period, we can be certain about the family origins of eight Templars[152] but of only two Hospitallers, and they were of the same kindred.[153] On the other hand, the fact that the backgrounds of so few masters can be firmly established suggests that family connections could play less of a part when it came to magistral elections than one might have supposed.

Chapter Four

TWO VERY DIFFERENT ORDERS

In a memorandum written in 1305 James of Molay, the last grand master of the Temple, asserted that "the Hospitallers were founded to care for the sick, and beyond that they bear arms . . . whereas the Templars were founded specifically for military service."[1] The Templars, in other words, were single minded. The Hospitallers were ambivalent. The Templars were committed to poverty as individuals, expressed in the image on their seal of two riders sharing a horse.[2] The Hospitallers were committed to the service of the poor themselves. The Templars fought out of love, because the need to defend Christians and the Holy Places demanded it. The Hospitallers fought out of love as an extension of their care of the poor. The admission rites of both orders made use of the unusual phrase "serf and slave." Serfs and slaves were unfree, serfs conditionally and slaves unconditionally, and their lords had rights of ownership over them. But whereas a Templar postulant was asked if he was prepared to live as a "serf and slave" of his order,[3] the Hospitaller promised to be "serf and slave" of his lords the sick.[4] So the Templars were owned by their order, the Hospitallers by their patients.

Growing in one case out of a company of secular knights and in the other from a breakaway group of Cassinese monks, the Temple and the Hospital helped create a new type of order, run by *fratres conversi*, in which the old distinctions between choir-monks and lay servitors were modified and in which, almost uniquely, the priests were never dominant.[5] The orders shared, of course, the duty of the service of prayer. Beyond that, the function of the Templars was to fight. That was what they had been founded by secular knights to do and it is not surprising that a strong military tone was pervasive. The Hospital had been established, on the other hand, to nurse and bury the poor. The promises every Hospitaller made contained no reference to warfare. If he fought, it was as an extension of his service to the poor. The maintenance of the great hospitals in Jerusalem and then in Acre, involving so many men and women and such great resources, meant that the Hospitallers could never have been as single minded as the Templars, even had they wanted to be; and once the direction their order would take had been settled around 1180 their ethos was always going to be less war-oriented. At least as well endowed as the Templars, they had to divert much of their income to meet the needs of their hospitals and the costs entailed in employing so many servants, which explains why they garrisoned fewer large castles.

In terms of membership the Temple, which was open to everyone from the richest noble to the poorest free peasant, was probably more representative of European society than the Hospital, the membership of which may have been drawn from a narrower base. The Temple admitted many more sergeants than did the Hospital, but because of the greater stress on military affairs and perhaps also through fear of being swamped by the sergeantry, the status of the Templar knights was elevated to a remarkable degree. The Hospital, in which there was a noticeably more relaxed attitude to caste, also had an important class of sisters.

The constitution of the Temple hardly developed over two centuries. The prerogatives of the grand masters and their convents counted for everything. The legislative powers of the chapters-general were limited, and there does not seem to have been any sustained attempt to seek western representation at them. On the other hand, some representatives of the western provinces came to the chapters-general of the Hospital, the statutes of which mattered a great deal and seem to have been widely circulated.

Having no practical function other than the defence of Christendom and still reflecting in many ways the governance of an eleventh-century Benedictine abbey, the Temple's institutional immaturity can be explained partly by the fact that effective warfare required unambiguous military leadership. But a consequence was that it never seems to have been locked into the conventional patterns of Church life that could have provided it with models for development. The nature of the Hospital's mission, the commitment to nursing as well as to the exercise of arms, placed it more in the mainstream and may have helped it to be more responsive to institutional adaptations occurring elsewhere in the Church. Putting it perhaps over-simply, while the Temple was in every sense a *nova religio*, founded to fulfil a role that was anything but conventional, the very ambiguity in the Hospital's mission conformed it more closely to the traditions of the Church. For all the problems in categorizing it, the Hospital was more recognizably a conventional religious order than was the Temple. This helps to explain on the one hand its ability to survive the crisis of the early fourteenth century and on the other the Temple's failure to do so.

— This raises the question why so many historians of the crusades and the Military Orders have treated the Temple and Hospital in the central Middle Ages as though they were sides to the same coin. There are, I think, two reasons for the assumptions they have made. First, they have interpreted the Hospital's early history in the light of its actions from the fourteenth to the eighteenth centuries. Its character altered after 1309, as we shall see. Secondly, most of the evidence for contemporary opinion dates from the last thirty years of the thirteenth century, when leading figures in Europe, focusing on the military needs of the Christian settlements in the Levant, were losing patience with the orders and were calling for their union. One of Pope Nicholas IV's first reactions to the fall of Acre in 1291 was to ask provincial councils to debate the merging of the orders,[6] although he died soon afterwards and nothing was done.[7]

From the early 1270s there was, in fact, a sense of impending disaster in the East. Contemporaries could not have failed to notice that, together with other religious institutions, the orders were transferring their archives overseas.[8] They had lost most of their castles and some of the wards of the hospital in Acre must have been empty as the flow of pilgrims dried up. As the threat to the city grew the Hospitallers converted part of a beautiful hall in their compound into water store, building in it two vast cisterns. They were still committed to assist in the defence of Acre and Tripoli, but after 1271 the only major castle they held was Margat. The Templars still had the responsibility of garrisoning Roche Guillaume, Tortosa, Sidon, and Chastel Pèlerin, but this was a substantially reduced commitment when compared to the relatively recent past. The orders may have decided to reduce the number of brothers-at-arms serving in the region, because in 1278 Pope Nicholas III reminded them that they must always keep sufficient military forces in the Holy Land.[9] The speeches and writings of this period, when those in responsible positions were thinking only of the measures that were needed to recover lost territory, were naturally concerned with military affairs to the exclusion of almost everything else, which explains why there are hardly any references in them to the Hospitallers' reputation for acts of mercy.[10]

The evidence is, therefore, misleading. I have already referred to the reactions of visitors to Acre and their impressions of the Hospitallers' work with the sick and the poor. And striking evidence that they were still famous for it is to be found in Jacquemart of Gielee's *Renart le Nouvel*, written ca. 1289, just before the fall of Acre. In this, one of the most popular and brilliantly funny of the Reynard the Fox epics, Jacquemart portrayed churchmen competing for Reynard's cynical and secular-minded patronage. The satire climaxed with the arrival in Rome of representatives of the Temple and the Hospital, who had come from Acre to offer Reynard a place in their respective convents. The Templar dwelt on the efforts of his brothers and the expenses they endured in the defence of Christendom. The Hospitaller maintained that his order caused as much damage to the Muslims as did the Temple, but he added that "in our hospital, which is full of charity, the wounded and the sick are healed, cured and cared for," and he argued that without Reynard's assistance sick pilgrims would have no hospital to go to. Jacquemart described the pope summing up the debate by confessing that he could not choose between the orders and in a farcical passage, that parodied the arguments for merging them, made Reynard decide to take the mastership of both.[11] But it is clear that the Hospital's dual mission had not been forgotten.

EPILOGUE

Between 1278 and 1283 the Hospitaller knight William of Santo Stefano was compiling a collection in translation of historical texts, with the help of the order's treasurer, who lent him material from the archives. William was transferred from Palestine to Lombardy, where he continued to add to his collection and wrote several treatises on the order's history and government. In 1299 he was promoted to the office of commander of Cyprus, but he had been replaced by 1303 and is not heard of again.[1]

He dismissed much of the nonsense on the prehistory of the Hospital that had been circulating for a century. In a passage that could almost have been written by a modern scholar he claimed to

> have discovered how our order began in histories which are
> accepted and believed to be authoritative by all men. It is said that
> there was a more ancient beginning . . . but that is not to be found
> in any authoritative source. . . . Now let us leave vanity and hold
> to the truth, for glorifying in lies is displeasing to God.[2]

Living at a time when, as we have seen, public opinion was much more concerned with the military contribution his order could make to the defence of what was left of the Christian holdings in the Levant than with its care of the sick, his writings nevertheless reveal how its twin aims—to care for the poor when they were sick and to wage war on their behalf, and by extension on behalf of Christendom—had been forged into a distinct mission.

He was engaged in his work of scholarship on the eve of a *cause célèbre* which had very different outcomes for the Hospitallers and the Templars. Within a decade the Templars would be arrested in a blaze of scandalous publicity and would be on the road to their suppression in 1312, after which most of their properties would pass into Hospitaller hands. Although it was not unknown for secular rulers to dissolve religious houses in their realms, it was very unusual for an order to be suppressed by the Church; it was, indeed, so rare an occurrence that when in 1646 the Piarists suffered this fate, contemporaries thought that the event was unprecedented.[3]

The common opinion that the Templars were innocent of all the charges levelled against them is now being challenged, and it is being suggested that in some commanderies postulants were forced into a blasphemous rite of passage involving the denial of Christ.[4] Whether the historians who are proposing this are right in their belief or not, the early fourteenth-century enquiries into the Temple revealed a system of government that had become old-fashioned and inefficient. Decisions affecting the whole order were being made by the grand master and his convent, who cannot have been *au fait* with events and developments in the western provinces because the masters hardly ever visited them and the provincials were not summoned to eastern chapters-general. Nevertheless, they had total legislative power and, as is so often to be found with autocracies, the result was spinelessness. One of the weaknesses in the ethos of the Military Orders was the way middle-ranking but noble brother knights tended to resist change and the authority of their superiors,[5] and a theme running through the responses of the Templar officials to interrogation was that they had habitually avoided monitoring the activities of their subordinates in case they should come across something inconvenient.[6]

The state of the Temple seems to have been so dire that one wonders how long it could have been allowed to remain in existence, with or without the scandal. It cannot be a coincidence that in the year 1309, when the investigation into the Templars was at its height, the Teutonic Knights and the Hospitallers took initiatives designed to demonstrate that they were still active and useful. The grand master of the Teutonic Order took up residence at Marienburg in Prussia, where it had been established for nearly a century,[7] and the Hospitallers moved their headquarters to the island of Rhodes, which they had invaded three years before. They were to hold it, together with all the Dodecanese, until 1522.[8] After losing it they went on to rule Malta from 1530 to 1798.[9]

In these order-states the sovereign rights of the Teutonic Order and the Hospital were always ambiguous. Prussia had been a principality, but no more than that, since 1226, and the grand master carried his prerogatives to Mergentheim, where he moved after the conversion of Prussia and Livonia into Lutheran duchies in the sixteenth century. Rhodes's standing was doubtful and Malta's was even more so, since it was a fief of the kingdom of Sicily. Stage by stage, however, the masters (now grand masters) of the Hospital assumed the attributes of sovereignty in a process that culminated in the adoption by Manoel Pinto (1741–73) of a closed crown.

Order-states had some similarities to the papal patrimonies in Italy and on the east bank of the Rhône, and to the Jesuit missionary settlements in South America. They were theocracies governed by an elite class of celibate soldier-religious, who originated from elsewhere and isolated themselves from the indigenous populations. Their policies towards their non-Christian neighbors, while theoretically defensive, were highly aggressive in practice and were exemplified by the *Reysen* of the Teutonic Knights, the caravans of the Rhodian and Maltese fleets, and the Hospitallers' use of licensed piracy, the *corso*.

The personality of the Hospital was bound to be affected by its new situation. It was ruling an independent territory and had built a small, but quite powerful, fleet. It obviously felt the need to respond to the criticism of its performance in the years leading up to the fall of Acre. It had inherited many of the Templar estates, and with them the attachment of Templar benefactors and their traditions. Its main hospital was now out-of-the-way, even if it was on a major sea-route to the East. The proportion of its income spent on the care of the sick must anyway have been declining from the 1270s onwards, as military and naval expenses swallowed up much of its revenue. Although there is a need for more research, one has the impression that from the fourteenth to the eighteenth centuries the Knights Hospitaller of St John, now called of Rhodes or of Malta, saw themselves more in the role of warriors than of nurses, and that the ambivalence that had prevailed in the twelfth and thirteenth centuries was less in evidence.

Nursing always remained a priority, however. The Hospitallers were building a hospital at Limassol, to which they had moved their headquarters, in 1296.[10] On their arrival on Rhodes in 1309 they at once established a temporary hospital, which between 1314 and 1356 was replaced by a purpose-built one. This gave way in 1440 to a magnificent new building[11] on which around 10 percent of their income was still being spent.[12] Their first act on being driven from Rhodes was to construct a tented hospital on a south Italian beach, and within three years of their arrival on Malta in 1530 they had built a hospital in Birgù. A great new infirmary was a desideratum in the planning of Valletta after 1565. This, the Sacred Infirmary, which could admit 563 patients, and in an emergency could be extended to take in 940, had sections devoted to pilgrims and members of religious communities, brother knights and convicts, and to fevers, wounds, and surgical cases, dysentery, mental illness, and contagious, venereal, and urinary diseases. The Hospitallers continued the ancient tradition of admitting all who needed treatment, whatever their religion, and they extended the range of their care to the resident Maltese population. They created a flourishing medical school, which was incorporated into their university in 1771. They also ran a hospital for women, an orphanage, a subsidiary hospital in Rabat, and a quarantine station, which was internationally regarded as the most efficient in the Mediterranean.[13]

It was this continuing tradition that provided the basis for the initiatives taken in the middle of the nineteenth century by Gottfried von Schröter, August von Haxthausen and others, when they revitalized the order's ancient mission of mercy.[14]

NOTES

Prologue

1. See Kaspar Elm, *Umbilicus Mundi* (Sint-Kruis, 1998), pp. 498–506; Christian Vogel, *Das Recht der Templer* (Münster, 2007), pp. 229–33.

2. Jonathan Riley-Smith, "Towards a History of the Military-Religious Orders," *The Hospitallers, the Mediterranean and Europe*, ed. Karl Borchardt, Nikolas Jaspert, and Helen Nicholson (Aldershot, 2007), p. 269.

3. D'Arcy Jonathan D. Boulton, *The Knights of the Crown* (Woodbridge, 1987), p. xviii and passim; Maurice Keen, *Chivalry* (New Haven and London, 1984), pp. 179–99.

4. The process is briefly described in Anthony Luttrell, "The Military Orders, 1312–1798," *The Oxford Illustrated History of the Crusades*, ed. Jonathan Riley-Smith (Oxford, 1995), pp. 348–50. See also Luis Adão Fonseca, "The Portuguese Military Orders and the Oceanic Navigations: From Piracy to Empire," *The Military Orders*, vol 4, *On Land and by Sea*, ed. Judith Upton-Ward (Aldershot, 2008), pp. 63–73. In England, King Henry VIII seems to have toyed with the idea of converting the grand priory of St John into an Order of the Crown with the function of defending Calais; Gregory O'Malley, *The Knights Hospitaller of the English Langue 1460–1565* (Oxford, 2005), pp. 179–84, 335.

5. See Luis Adão Fonseca, "As Ordens Militares e a Expansão," *A Alta Nobreza e a Fundação do Estado da Índia* (Lisbon, 2004), pp. 325–47; Luis Adão Fonseca, "La storiografia dell'espansione marittima portoghese (secc. XIV–XV)," *Bullettino dell'Istituto Storico Italiano per il Medio Evo* 106 (2004), 299–346; Isabel Morgado S. E. Silva and Maria Cristina Pimenta, "As Ordens de Santiago e de Cristo e a Fundação do Estado da Índia: Uma Perspectiva de Estudo," *A Alta Nobreza e a Fundação do Estado da Índia* (Lisbon, 2004), pp. 349–87.

6. Riley-Smith, "Towards a History," pp. 270–73.

7. For surveys of this period, see Malcolm Barber, *The New Knighthood: A History of the Order of the Temple* (Cambridge, 1994); Alain Demurger, *Les Templiers: Une chevalerie chrétienne au moyen âge* (Paris, 2005); Pierre-Vincent Claverie, *L'Ordre du Temple en Terre Sainte et à Chypre au XIIIe siècle*, 3 vols (Nicosia, 2005); Jonathan Riley-Smith, *The Knights of St John in Jerusalem and Cyprus, c. 1050–1310* (London, 1967).

8. For recent examples, see Jochen Burgtorf, *The Central Convent of Hospitallers and Templars. History, Organization, and Personnel (1099/1120–1310)* (Leiden and Boston, 2008); Pierre Bonneaud, *Le prieuré de Catalogne, le couvent de Rhodes et la couronne d'Aragon 1415–1447* (Millau, 2004); Michael Gervers, *The Hospitaller Cartulary in the British Library (Cotton MS Nero E VI)* (Toronto, 1981); Michael Gervers, "Pro defensione Terre Sancte: The Development and Exploitation of the Hospitallers' Landed Estate in Essex," *The Military Orders: Fighting for the Faith and Caring for the Sick*, ed. Malcolm Barber (Aldershot, 1994), pp. 3–20; Anthony Luttrell and Léon Pressouyre, eds., *La Commanderie, institution des ordres militaires dans l'Occident médiéval* (Paris, 2002); David Marcombe, *Leper Knights* (Woodbridge, 2003); Kristjan Toomaspoeg, *Templari e ospitalieri nella Sicilia medievale* (Taranto, 2003); Damien Carraz, *L'ordre du Temple dans la basse vallée du Rhône, 1124–1312: Ordres militaires, croisades et sociétés méridionales* (Lyons, 2005), pp. 191–418; Judith Bronstein, *The Hospitallers and the Holy Land: Financing the Latin East 1187–1274* (Woodbridge, 2005).

9. Exceptions are Giles Constable, "The Place of the Crusader in Medieval Society," *Viator* 29 (1998), pp. 392–403; Tom Licence, "The Military Orders as Monastic Orders," *Crusades* 5 (2006), pp. 39–53; Simonetta Cerrini (ed.), *I Templari, la guerra et la santità* (Rimini, 2000), p. 7. See also Simonetta Cerrini, *La Révolution des Templiers* (Paris, 2007), pp. 17–18; Alan Forey, *The Military Orders* (Basingstoke, 1992), pp. 1–3.

10. Laurent H. Cottineau, *Répertoire topo-bibliographique des abbayes et prieurés*, 3 vols (Mâcon, 1935–70).

11. David Knowles and R. Neville Hadcock, *Medieval Religious Houses: England and Wales* (London, 1971), p. xiii.

12. See Helen Nicholson, *Templars, Hospitallers and Teutonic Knights: Images of the Military Orders 1128–1291* (Leicester, 1993), passim.

13. Alan Forey, "The Military Orders in the Crusading Proposals of the Late-Thirteenth and Early-Fourteenth Centuries," *Traditio* 36 (1980), pp. 317–45; Forey, *The Military Orders*, pp. 216–20; Claverie, *L'Ordre du Temple en Terre Sainte*, 2.207–27.

14. Most of the material is to be found in *Cartulaire général de l'ordre des Hospitaliers de St Jean de Jérusalem (1100–1310)*, ed. Joseph Delaville Le Roulx, 4 vols (Paris, 1894–1906) (hereafter *Cart Hosp*), passim. See also Anthony Lut-

trell, "The Hospitallers' Early Written Records," *The Crusades and their Sources,* ed. John France and William G. Zajac (Aldershot, 1998), pp. 135–54.

15. Seven of the original charters from the archive survive, published in *Codice diplomatico del sacro militare ordine Gerosolimitano oggi di Malta,* ed. Sebastiano Paoli, 2 vols (Lucca, 1733–37), 1.40–41, 206–7, 250; *Les Archives, la bibliothèque et le trésor de l'ordre de Saint- Jean de Jérusalem à Malte,* ed. Joseph Delaville Le Roulx (Paris, 1883), pp. 112–13, 134–35, 181–84; and "Chartes de Terre Sainte," ed. Joseph Delaville Le Roulx, *ROL* 11 (1905–8), pp. 183–84. A further six calendar entries were compiled in Provence in 1741: *Cart Hosp* 2.907; "Inventaire des pièces de Terre Sainte de l'ordre de l'Hôpital," ed. Joseph Delaville Le Roulx, *ROL* 3 (1895), pp. 62, 68, 86, 94; *Papsturkunden für Templer und Johanniter,* ed. Rudolf Hiestand, 2 vols, Vorarbeiten zum Oriens Pontificius 2 (Göttingen, 1972–84), 2.262–63. A number of papal letters were copied into a fifteenth-century French Hospitaller *bullarium* (National Library of Malta, Archives of the Order of St John: Arch 1128 [*Bullarium rubeum*]). See *Papsturkunden für Templer und Johanniter* 1.401–2, 413–14; *Malteser Urkunden und Regesten zur Geschichte der Tempelherren und der Johanniter,* ed. Hans Prutz (Munich, 1883), passim. Copies of two other papal letters were entered into a sixteenth-century collection in Poitiers, which may have been an inventory of the Hospitallers' local archive in Paris (Rudolf Hiestand, "Zum Problem des Templerzentralarchivs," *Archivalische Zeitschrift* 76 [1980], pp. 27–29, 31). Another important charter, the confirmation in 1157 of the gift of the castle of Tortosa in Syria, was copied in Spain in 1377 for the Order of Montesa ("The Templars and the Castle of Tortosa in Syria," ed. Jonathan Riley-Smith, *English Historical Review* 84 [1969], pp. 284–88). Some, but not all, of these charters must have passed into Hospitaller hands as the deeds of properties acquired in exchanges. Rudolf Hiestand ("Zum Problem," pp. 36–38), with the support of Burgtorf (*The Central Convent,* p. 7), has suggested that the archive was transferred to the Hospitallers on Cyprus and was lost with the island in 1571, but I am inclined to believe that it was in Europe until at least the fifteenth century.

16. Vogel, *Das Recht,* pp. 305–8. Claverie (*L'Ordre du Temple en Terre Sainte* 1.136–41) thinks he has identified thirteen chapters-general, but there is good evidence for only one before 1291, in 1262, although no statutes can be associated with it. Jonathan Riley-Smith, "An Ignored Meeting of a Templar Chapter-General," *Prof. Dr. Iflin Demirkent Anisina,* ed. Abdülkerim Özaydin et al. (Istanbul, 2008), pp. 389–93.

17. Vogel, *Das Recht,* pp. 69–71, 85, 102–38. For the manuscripts, see Vogel, *Das Recht,* pp. 69–102; Simonetta Cerrini, "La tradition manuscrite de la Règle du Temple," *Autour de la Première Croisade,* ed. Michel Balard (Paris, 1996), pp. 203–18; Cerrini, *La Révolution,* pp. 120–88; Alois Knöpfler, "Die

Ordensregel der Tempelherren," *Historisches Jahrbuch* 8 (1887), pp. 691–95; *The Catalan Rule of the Templars*, ed. Judith Upton-Ward (Woodbridge, 2003), passim. I am not convinced by the rationale for the state of Templar legislation provided by Burgtorf, *The Central Convent*, pp. 11–12.

18. *Le procès des Templiers*, ed. Jules Michelet, 2 vols (Paris, 1841–51) (hereafter *Procès*), 2.277–420; Heinrich Finke, *Papsttum und Untergang des Templerordens*, 2 vols (Berlin, 1907), 2.313–24, 328–40, 342–64; Hans Prutz, *Entwicklung und Untergang des Tempelherrenordens* (Berlin, 1888), pp. 324–26, 334–35, 338–39; Konrad Schottmüller, *Der Untergang des Templer-Ordens*, 2 vols (Berlin, 1887), 2.14–71; "Inquesta dominorum Commissariorum Clementis pape in Castro de Caynone diocesis Turonensis," ed. Barbara Frale, *Il papato e il processo ai Templari: L'inedita assoluzione di Chinon alla luce della diplomatica pontificia* (Rome, 2003), pp. 198–214.

19. *Le procès des Templiers d'Auvergne, 1310–1311*, ed. Roger Sève and Anne-Marie Chagny-Sève (Paris, 1986), pp. 93–263; Léon Menard, *Histoire civile, ecclésiastique et littéraire de la ville de Nismes*, 7 vols (Paris, 1750) 1 Preuves, pp. 166–219; *Monuments historiques relatifs à la condamnation des chevaliers du Temple et à l'abolition de leur ordre*, ed. François-Just-Marie Raynouard (Paris, 1813), pp. 268–70, 280–84; *The Trial of the Templars in the Papal State and the Abruzzi*, ed. Anne Gilmour-Bryson (Vatican City, 1982), pp. 65–262; "Dei Tempieri e del loro processo in Toscana," ed. Telesforo Bini, *Atti della Reale Accademia Lucchese di Scienze, Lettere ed Arti* 13 (1845), pp. 460–501; "Interrogatorio di Templari in Cesena (1310)," ed. Francesco Tommasi, *Acri 1291: Le fine della presenza degli ordini militari in Terra Santa e i nuovi orientamenti nel XIV secolo*, ed. Francesco Tommasi (Perugia, 1996), pp. 287–98; Schottmüller, *Der Untergang* 2.78–102, 108–39, 147–400; "L'inedito processo del Templari in Castiglia (Medina del Campo, 27 Aprile 1310)," ed. Josep Maria Sans i Travé, *Acri 1291: Le fine della presenza degli ordini militari in Terra Santa e i nuovi orientamenti nel XIV secolo*, ed. Francesco Tommasi (Perugia, 1996), pp. 249–64; Fidel Fita y Colomé, *Siete concilios españoles* (Madrid, 1882), pp. 78–110; *Procès* 2.424–515; Finke, *Papsttum* 2.364–79; *Conciliae Magni Britannie et Hibernie*, ed. David Wilkins, 3 vols (London, 1737) 2.334–400. See also Alan Forey, *The Fall of the Templars in the Crown of Aragon* (Aldershot, 2001), passim; Aurea Javierre Mur, "Aportacion al estudio del proceso contra el Temple en Castilla," *Revista des Archivos, Bibliotecas y Museos* 69 (1961), pp. 75–100.

20. *Procès* 1.1–648; 2.1–274.

21. For the earliest period, see *Cartulaires des Templiers de Douzens*, ed. Pierre Gérard and Elisabeth Magnou (Paris, 1965); *Records of the Templars in England in the Twelfth Century: The Inquest of 1185*, ed. Beatrice A. Lees (London, 1935); Gervers, *The Hospitaller Cartulary*.

22. Jonathan Riley-Smith, "The Origins of the Commandery in the Temple and the Hospital," *La Commanderie, Institution des ordres militaires dans l'Occident médiéval*, ed. Anthony Luttrell and Léon Pressouyre (Paris, 2002), pp. 9–18; Alan Forey, *The Templars in the Corona de Aragón* (London, 1973), passim.

23. Barbara Frale has suggested that the western provinces could even constitute an alternative source of authority; see her *I Templari* (Bologna, 2004), pp. 115–20

24. Jonathan Riley-Smith, "The Military Orders and the East, 1149–1291," *Knighthoods of Christ*, ed. Norman Housley (Aldershot, 2007), pp. 137–49.

25. *Cart Hosp* 4.292.

26. Cerrini, *La Révolution*, pp. 34–35; Tom Licence, "The Templars and the Hospitallers, Christ and the Saints," *Crusades* 4 (2005), pp. 53–54; Francesco Tommasi, "Per i rapporti tra Templari e Cistercensi: Orientamenti a indirizzi di ricerca," *I Templari: Una vita tra riti cavallereschi e fedaltà all Chiesa*, ed. Goffredo Viti (Florence, 1995), pp. 264–65.

27. *Les Légendes de l'Hôpital de Saint-Jean de Jérusalem*, ed. Antoine Calvet (Paris, 2000), pp. 122–24, 134–36; Anthony Luttrell, "Iconography and Historiography: The Italian Hospitallers before 1530," *Sacra Militia* 3 (2002), pp. 41–44; Licence, "The Templars," pp. 55–57; Anthony Luttrell, "The Skull of Blessed Gerard," *The Order's Early Legacy in Malta*, ed. John Azzopardi (Valletta, 1989), p. 45; Anthony Luttrell, "The Hospitallers' Medical Tradition," *The Military Orders: Fighting for the Faith and Caring for the Sick*, ed. Malcolm Barber (Aldershot, 1994), pp. 74–75. In the fourteenth century there was Flore (or Fleur), a sister at the nunnery at Beaulieu, whose cult developed soon after her death in 1347. For the Hospital's calendar, see Anne-Marie Legras and Jean-Loup Lemaître, "La pratique liturgique des Templiers et des Hospitaliers de Saint-Jean de Jérusalem," *L'Ecrit dans la société médiévale: Divers aspects de sa pratique du XIe à XVe siècle*, ed. Caroline Bourlet and Annie Dufour (Paris, 1993), pp. 89–94, 110–13.

28. The reputation of Hugh of Payns, the founder of the Templars, could have suffered in this way, although the brothers may have preserved his head as a relic. Finke, *Papsttum* 2.335; Licence, "The Templars," p. 53.

29. "Les Chemins et les Pelerinages de la Terre Sainte," ed. Henri Michelant and Gaston Raynaud, *Itinéraires à Jérusalem et descriptions de la Terre Sainte rédigés en français* (Geneva, 1882), p. 199; The Templar of Tyre, *Cronaca del Templare di Tiro (1243–1314)*, ed. Laura Minervini (Naples, 2000), p. 104. See Jonathan Riley-Smith, "The Death and Burial of Latin Christian Pilgrims to Jerusalem and Acre, 1099–1291," *Crusades* 7 (2008), pp. 176–77; Jonathan Riley-Smith, "The Crown of France and Acre, 1254–1291," *France and the Holy Land*, ed. Daniel Weiss and Lisa Mahoney (Baltimore and London, 2004), p. 51.

30. *Acta Sanctorum. October* 4.363.

One   THE ESTABLISHMENT OF TRADITIONS

1. "Narratio de primordiis ordinis Theutonici," ed. Max Perlbach, *Die Statuten des Deutschen Ordens* (Halle, 1890), pp. 159–60; Innocent III, *Die Register*, ed. Othmar Hageneder et al., 7 vols so far (Graz/Cologne/Rome/Vienna, 1964–) 1.823.

2. *La continuation de Guillaume de Tyr (1184–97)*, ed. M. Ruth Morgan (Paris, 1982), p. 99. See Anthony Luttrell, "The Hospitaller Background of the Teutonic Order," *Religiones militares*, ed. Anthony Luttrell and Francesco Tommasi (Città di Castello, 2008), pp. 27–41; Marie-Luise Favreau, *Studien zur Frühgeschichte des Deutschen Ordens* (Stuttgart, 1975), passim.

3. See Cerrini, *La Révolution*, pp. 75–84; Pierre-Vincent Claverie, "Les débuts de l'ordre du Temple en Orient," *Le moyen âge* 111 (2005), pp. 546–57.

4. See Barber, *The New Knighthood*, pp. 6–10; Anthony Luttrell, "The Earliest Templars," *Autour de la première croisade*, ed. Michel Balard (Paris, 1996), pp. 193–202; Cerrini, *La Révolution*, pp. 37–39; Kaspar Elm, "Kanoniker und Ritter vom Heiligen Grab," *Die geistlichen Ritterorden Europas*, ed. Josef Fleckenstein and Manfred Hellmann (Sigmaringen, 1980), pp. 159–65; Vogel, *Das Recht*, pp. 27–32.

5. Benjamin Kedar, "On the Origins of the Earliest Laws of Frankish Jerusalem: The Canons of the Council of Nablus, 1120," *Speculum* 74 (1999), p. 334.

6. Denys Pringle, *The Churches of the Crusader Kingdom of Jerusalem: A Corpus*, 4 vols (Cambridge, 1993–2009), 3.420–22. See Jonathan Riley-Smith, *The First Crusaders, 1095–1131* (Cambridge, 1997), p. 170.

7. *Le Cartulaire du chapitre du Saint-Sépulcre de Jérusalem*, ed. Geneviève Bresc-Bautier (Paris, 1984), pp. 157–58, 262; Claverie, "Les débuts," p. 548.

8. See Anthony Luttrell, "Templari e ospitalieri: alcuni confronti," *I Templari, la guerra e la santità*, ed. Simonetta Cerrini (Rimini, 2000), pp. 143–45; Luttrell, "The Earliest Templars," p. 198.

9. Riley-Smith, *The First Crusaders*, pp. 162–63.

10. *Die ursprüngliche Templerregel*, ed. Gustav Schnürer (Freiburg im Breisgau, 1903), passim; Cerrini, *La Révolution*, pp. 100–134. See Rudolf Hiestand, "Kardinalbischof Matthäus von Albano, das Konzil von Troyes und die Entstehung des Templerordens," *Zeitschrift für Kirchengeschichte* 99 (1988), pp. 295–325; Vogel, *Das Recht*, pp. 36–38; also Réginald Grégoire, "La spiritualità Templare," *I Templari: Una vita tra riti cavallereschi e fedaltà all Chiesa*, ed. Goffredo Viti (Florence, 1995), pp. 201–15. For the Temple's relationship with the Cistercians, see Francesco Tommasi, "Per i rapporti," pp. 227–74; Vogel, *Das Recht*, pp. 32–33, 57–58.

11. "Hugh Peccator," ed. Jean Leclercq, "Un document sur les débuts des Templiers," *Revue d'histoire ecclésiastique* 52 (1957), pp. 86–89. It is not clear whether this individual was the founder himself or the famous canon of the

priory of St Victor in Paris. Claims are now being made for the former; Cerrini, *La Révolution*, pp. 45–47.

12. *Lettres des premiers Chartreux*, ed. a Carthusian, vol 1 (Paris, 1962), pp. 154–60.

13. *Papsturkunden für Templer und Johanniter* 2.96–103. See Vogel, *Das Recht*, pp. 38–40.

14. Bernard of Clairvaux, "De laude novae militiae ad milites Templi liber," *Sancti Bernardi Opera*, ed. Jean Leclercq et al. 8 vols (Rome, 1963), 3.212–39. See Inos Biffi, "La figura di Cristo e i 'Loca Sancta' nelle vita dei Templari," *I Templari: Una vita tra riti cavallereschi e fedaltà all Chiesa*, ed. Goffredo Viti (Florence, 1995), pp. 19–29.

15. *Procès* 1.389.

16. Schottmüller, *Der Untergang*, 2.67; *Procès* 1.615–16; 2.223, 228, 231, 232.

17. "Hugh Peccator," p. 87.

18. *Die ursprüngliche Templerregel*, p. 147; "Hugh Peccator," p. 87; Bernard of Clairvaux, "De laude," pp. 214–15, 217–19.

19. *Papsturkunden für Templer und Johanniter* 2.96.

20. *Die ursprüngliche Templerregel*, pp. 135–36; "Hugh Peccator," p. 89; Bernard of Clairvaux, "De laude," pp. 214–24.

21. Jonathan Riley-Smith, *The First Crusade and the Idea of Crusading* (London, 1986), pp. 118–19.

22. Riley-Smith, *The First Crusade and the Idea of Crusading*, pp. 135–52; Riley-Smith, *The First Crusaders*, pp. 68–70. See also Jonathan Riley-Smith, *The Crusades, Christianity, and Islam* (New York, 2008), pp. 29–44.

23. Thomas Aquinas, *Summa Theologiae* 2a2ae, qu. 188, art. 3.

24. William Purkis, *Crusading Spirituality in the Holy Land and Iberia, c.1095–c.1187* (Woodbridge, 2008), pp. 101–11.

25. *Papsturkunden für Templer und Johanniter* 2.99.

26. Jacquemart Gielee, *Renart le Nouvel*, ed. Henri Roussel (Paris, 1961), p. 310.

27. *Procès*, passim.

28. Isaac of L'Etoile, *Sermons*, ed. Anselme Hoste and Gaetano Raciti, 3 vols (Paris, 1967–87), 3.158–60.

29. Although Hospitaller martyrologies were popular in the seventeenth century. See for example Mathieu de Goussancourt, *Le Martyrologie des Chevaliers de St Jean de Jérusalem*, 2 vols (Paris, 1643).

30. Angel Manrique, in *Annales Cistercienses*, 4 vols (Lyons, 1613–59), 3.97, provided a garbled account that confused the capture of the Templar grand master in the battle of Marj Ayun with the fall of Vadum Jacob. Cf. Tommasi, "Per i rapporti," pp. 260–61.

31. Fidenzio of Padua, "Liber recuperationis Terrae Sanctae," ed. Girolamo Gulobovich, *Biblioteca Bio-Bibliografica della Terra Santa e dell'Oriente*

Francescano, 18 vols (Florence, 1906–48), 2.24–25; *Biblioteca Bio-Bibliografica della Terra Santa*, comp. Gulobovich, 1.260–61, 264; The Templar of Tyre, *Cronaca*, p. 110; *Procès* 1.170–71; Schottmüller, *Der Untergang* 2.162, 387.

32. *Cart Hosp* 2.559. But according to William of Santo Stefano ("Recueil," Bibl. Nat. Ms fr. Anciens fonds no. 6049, f. 140r) the sermon was heard before Mass.

33. James of Vitry, "Sermo XXXVII ad fratres ordinis militaris, insignitos charactere Militiae Christi," ed. Jean-Baptiste Pitra, *Analecta Novissima Spicilegii Solesmensis Altera Continuatio*, 2 vols. (Paris, 1885–88), 2.405–14. Referring to the order's seal, James commented that two proud men could not ride on one saddle.

34. James of Vitry "Sermo XXXVIII," p. 420. It is clear from internal evidence that both sermons were addressed to the Templars.

35. The translation of their Rule into French, dated by Simonetta Cerrini to ca. 1150, marked in her view a dilution of the original spirituality in its greater practicality and in its expression of popular ideas such as vengeance. Cerrini, *La Révolution*, pp. 195–218.

36. And even beyond. See Riley-Smith, *The Crusades, Christianity, and Islam*, pp. 45–61.

37. James of Vitry believed that the Hospital had imitated the Temple in adopting a military wing; see his "Historia orientalis seu Hierosolymitana," ed. Jacques Bongars, *Gesta Dei per Francos* (Hannau, 1611), p. 1084.

38. Burgtorf, *The Central Convent*, p. 34.

39. *Papsturkunden für Templer und Johanniter* 2.196.

40. Elm, *Umbilicus Mundi*, p. 502.

41. Rudolf Hiestand, "Die Anfänge der Johanniter," *Die geistlichen Ritterorden Europas*, ed. Josef Fleckenstein and Manfred Hellmann (Sigmaringen, 1980), pp. 33–37; Riley-Smith, *The Knights of St John*, pp. 32–52.

42. Riley-Smith, *The First Crusaders*, pp. 163–64. See Riley-Smith, *The Knights of St John*, pp. 52–54; Hiestand, "Die Anfänge der Johanniter," pp. 64–78. No evidence for a brother knight can be found before 1148 and the reference is a doubtful one. "Fragment d'un cartulaire de l'ordre de Saint Lazare en Terre-Sainte," ed. Arthur de Marsy, *AOL 2* (1884), p. 127. See *Cart Hosp* 1.129 of 1144 for a Petrus Lupus *miles*, but he appears among a list of *confratres*.

43. The earliest recruit from a major family, Count Robert II of Auvergne, had entered by 1141. *Cart Hosp* 1.113, 118. But cf. Burgtorf, *The Central Convent*, p. 62.

44. *Papsturkunden für Templer und Johanniter* 2.222–30.

45. "De primordiis et inventione sacrae religionis Jerosolymitanae" and "Primordium et origo sari xenodochii atque ordinis militiae Sancto Johannis Baptistae Hospitalariorum Hierososolimitani (Le fondement du s. hospital et

de l'ordre de la chevalerie de S. Jehan Baptiste de Jerusalem)," in "Exordium Hospitalariorum," *RHC Oc* 5.429, 431, 435.

46. None, indeed, until an agreement with Duke Bela III of Hungary in the 1160s, which contains a clause covering the possibility of his sons wanting to serve the order and being lent horses and arms. *Cart Hosp* 1.222.

47. *Cart Hosp* 1.6–8, 71; 4.243. Para-crusaders sometimes ended up joining one of the military orders. Riley-Smith, *The First Crusaders*, pp. 158–60.

48. *Papsturkunden für Templer und Johanniter* 2.159–60, and see 2.150–51. Forey, *The Military Orders*, pp. 20–21.

49. Ernoul, "L'Estat de la Cité de Iherusalem," ed. Henri Michelant and Gaston Raynaud, *Itinéraires à Jérusalem et descriptions de la Terre Sainte rédigés en français* (Geneva, 1882), p. 41.

50. Riley-Smith, *The Knights of St John*, pp. 69–73; Burgtorf, *The Central Convent*, pp. 65–72; Richard P. Harper and Denys Pringle, *Belmont Castle* (Oxford, 2000), passim; Denys Pringle, *Secular Buildings in the Crusader Kingdom of Jerusalem: An Archaeological Gazetteer* (Cambridge, 1997), pp. 32–33, 96; Adrian Boas, *Archaeology of the Military Orders* (London, 2006), pp. 228–30.

51. *Papsturkunden für Templer und Johanniter* 2.222–30.

52. *Cart Hosp* 1.360–61.

53. *Papsturkunden für Templer und Johanniter* 2.159–62. Hiestand's commentary is on 2.136–59, esp. 2.150–51.

54. *Cart Hosp* 1.429.

55. *Cart Hosp* 1.426.

56. "A Twelfth-Century Description of the Jerusalem Hospital," ed. Benjamin Kedar, *The Military Orders*, vol 2, *Welfare and Warfare*, ed. Helen Nicholson (Aldershot, 1998), pp. 21–22.

57. Pringle, *The Churches* 3.228–36.

58. Pringle, *The Churches* 3.222–28; also Adrian Boas, *Jerusalem in the Time of the Crusades* (London and New York, 2001), pp. 185–87.

59. Pringle, *The Churches* 1.7–17, 239–50.

60. "A Twelfth-Century Description," ed. Kedar, pp. 18–26; "Administrative Regulations for the Hospital of St John in Jerusalem dating from the 1180s," ed. Susan Edgington, *Crusades* 4 (2005), pp. 21–37

61. Piers Mitchell, *Medicine in the Crusades: Warfare, Wounds and the Medieval Surgeon* (Cambridge, 2004), pp. 46–107; Susan Edgington, "Medical Care in the Hospital of St John in Jerusalem," *The Military Orders*, vol 2, *Welfare and Warfare*, ed. Helen Nicholson (Aldershot, 1998), pp. 27–33. Byzantine and Muslim hospitals had a range of specialized wards as well as general ones. We have definite knowledge of only one specialized ward—for obstetrics—in Jerusalem, although there is a hint that there was another, for intensive care, in "Administrative Regulations," ed. Edgington, p. 32.

62. The old conception that Western medicine was greatly inferior to Eastern is now considered to be an exaggeration. The latest and most informed opinion is that in surgery "there is little evidence to suggest that typical practice by crusaders, Frankish settlers or indigenous Christians, Jews and Muslims was dramatically different"; Mitchell, *Medicine*, pp. 180–81.

63. "Administrative Regulations," ed. Edgington, p. 32.

64. Mitchell, *Medicine*, pp. 105–6.

65. *Cart Hosp* 1.425–29; "Administrative Regulations," ed. Edgington, pp. 24–36; "A Twelfth-Century Description," ed. Kedar, pp. 13–26.

66. "A Twelfth-Century Description," ed. Kedar, p. 18.

67. *Cart Hosp* 1.428; "Administrative Regulations," ed. Edgington, p. 28.

68. "A Twelfth-Century Description," ed. Kedar, p. 20.

69. "Administrative Regulations," ed. Edgington, p. 28.

70. *Les Légendes*, pp. 122, 134, 144, 153.

71. "A Twelfth-Century Description," ed. Kedar, p. 18.

72. *Cart Hosp* 1.121–22; Pringle, *The Churches* 3.222–28; Boas, *Jerusalem*, pp. 185–87. For the dedication of the church, see Theoderic, "Peregrinatio," ed. Robert Huygens, *Peregrinationes tres*, CCCM 139 (Turnhout, 1994), pp. 146–47.

73. See Jaroslav Folda, *The Art of the Crusaders in the Holy Land, 1098–1187* (Cambridge, 1995), pp. 130–286.

74. *Cart Hosp* 1.113–15, 135–36; *Cartulaire du chapitre du Saint-Sépulcre*, pp. 226–28; Pringle, *The Churches* 1.7–17; Folda, *The Art of the Crusaders*, pp. 382–90. M. Ehlich has challenged the view that the settlers ever considered this site to be Emmaus; "The Identification of Emmaus with Abū Gōš Reconsidered," *Zeitschrift des deutschen Palästinavereins* 112 (1996), pp. 165–69.

75. *Papsturkunden für Kirchen im Heiligen Lande*, ed. Rudolf Hiestand, Vorarbeiten zum Oriens Pontificius 3 (Göttingen, 1985), p. 170. See Favreau, *Studien*, pp. 12–34.

76. See *Papsturkunden für Templer und Johanniter* 2.104–35.

77. William of Tyre, *Chronicon*, ed. Robert Huygens, 2 parts, CCCM 63, 63A (Turnhout, 1986), pp. 812–20. See Riley-Smith, *The Knights of St John*, pp. 398–400.

78. William of Tyre, *Chronicon*, pp. 812–13. According to John of Würzburg ("Peregrinatio," ed. Robert Huygens, *Peregrinationes tres*, CCCM 139 [Turnhout, 1994] p. 131) it was "beautiful."

79. *Cart Hosp* 1.148–49.

80. See Jonathan Riley-Smith, "Further Thoughts on the Layout of the Hospital in Acre," *Chemins d'outre-mer*, ed. Damien Coulon, Catherine Otten-Froux, Paul Pagès, and Dominique Valérien, 2 vols (Paris, 2004), 2.758.

81. Riley-Smith, "The Death and Burial of Latin Christian Pilgrims," pp. 177–78.

82. *Cart Hosp* 1.437–38.

83. *Cart Hosp* 2.231–34, 238–40, 856.

84. *Cart Hosp* 3.180.

85. "Inventaire et comptes de la succession d'Eudes, comte de Nevers (Acre 1266)," ed. Alphonse-Martial Chazaud, *Mémoires de la société des antiquaires de France*, sér. 4, 2 (1871), p. 200. There survive the records of gifts to the hospital by pilgrims, crusaders and residents of the kingdom: *Cart Hosp* 2.231–34, 248–49, 293–94, 581–82, 750–51, 779–81, 856; also *Cart Hosp* 2.287–88; 3.180. Some charters issued on behalf of men who must have been patients—although of the richer sort—survive: *Cart Hosp* 2.41–42, 168, 298, 308–9; 3.91–92. An extraordinary story of a Muslim sultan's endowment of the hospital seems to have been widespread in the west; Matthew Paris, *Chronica maiora*, ed. Henry R. Luard, 7 vols, Rolls Series 57 (London, 1872–83), 3.486; *Récits d'un ménestral de Reims*, ed. Natalis de Wailly (Paris, 1876), pp. 104–9.

86. *La Règle du Temple*, ed. Henri de Curzon (Paris, 1886), p. 344. See *Procès* 2.19, 21.

87. Riley-Smith, *The Knights of St John*, p. 233.

88. Riley-Smith, *The Knights of St John*, pp. 124–43. Perhaps a list of regulations on military discipline similar to the surviving instructions for the operation of their hospital in Jerusalem, which comprise a sort of handbook drawn from mostly lost statutes, has disappeared. See "Administrative Regulations," ed. Edgington, pp. 24–36. See also Katja Klement, "Alcune osservazioni sul Vat. Lat. 4852," *Studi Melitensi* 3 (1995), pp. 242–43.

Two Communities

1. Fidenzio of Padua, pp. 24–25.

2. *Cart Hosp* 4.292.

3. Christopher Marshall, *Warfare in the Latin East, 1192–1291* (Cambridge, 1992), pp. 222–23.

4. Barber, *The New Knighthood*, p. 232; Riley-Smith, *The Knights of St John*, p. 88.

5. Barber, *The New Knighthood*, pp. 129, 160–61, 232, 376; Riley-Smith, *The Knights of St John*, p. 137 note.

6. About one hundred of these were captured, including both masters and the marshal of the Temple; Matthew Paris, *Chronica maiora* 4.301. See Jonathan Riley-Smith's notes to *Ayyubids, Mamlukes and Crusaders: Selections from the Tarikh al-Duwal wa'l Muluk of Ibn al-Furat*, ed. Ursula Lyons and Malcolm C. Lyons, 2 vols (Cambridge, 1971), 2.173–75.

7. *Cart Hosp* 3.115; Riley-Smith's notes to *Ayyubids, Mamlukes and Crusaders* 2.207–8.

8. Claverie, *L'Ordre du Temple en Terre Sainte* 2.100–103.

9. Riley-Smith, "The Military Orders and the East," passim.

10. *Flores historiarum*, ed. Henry R. Luard, 3 vols, Rolls Series 95 (London, 1890), 2.451–52.

11. The letter has been dated to 1261, but it must have been written in 1260 because it contains no reference to the battle of 'Ayn Jalut and the list of Templar castles does not include Sidon and Beaufort. Written on 4 March, it was in the hands of Guy of Basainville, the order's visitor-general in France, by 18 June. "Annales monasterii Burtonensis," ed. Henry R. Luard, *Annales Monastici*, 5 vols, Rolls Series 36 (London, 1864–69) 1.491–95; *Monumentorum Boicorum collectio nova*, ed. Accademia scientiarum Boica, 29 ii (Munich, 1831), pp. 197–202. For the events, see R. Stephen Humphreys, *From Saladin to the Mongols: The Ayyubids of Damascus, 1193–1260* (Albany, 1977), pp. 337–63.

12. *Cart Hosp* 3.541. The master also reported the loss of one hundred war-horses and arms worth more than fifteen hundred silver marks.

13. Bronstein, *The Hospitallers*, pp. 11–12, 138.

14. Matthew Paris, *Chronica maiora* 3.404–6. Bronstein, *The Hospitallers*, p. 21. See also Barber, *The New Knighthood*, pp. 232, 376; Vogel, *Das Recht*, p. 43.

15. *Procès* 1.143

16. *Procès* 2.139.

17. Schottmüller, *Der Untergang* 2.47.

18. Schottmüller, *Der Untergang* 2.59.

19. *Procès* 2.400.

20. *Procès* 2.221–22.

21. Schottmüller, *Der Untergang* 2.132; *Procès* 2.146–47.

22. Alan Forey, "Towards a Profile of the Templars in the Early Fourteenth Century," *The Military Orders. Fighting for the Faith and Caring for the Sick*, ed. Malcolm Barber (Aldershot, 1994), pp. 200–202. See also Claverie, *L'Ordre du Temple en Terre Sainte* 1.188–90.

23. Riley-Smith, *The Knights of St John*, pp. 280–82.

24. "Inquesta," ed. Frale, p. 208.

25. *Procès* 1.409–10.

26. *Procès* 2.298. For his kinship with Adam, see *Procès* 1.501.

27. *Procès* 1.415.

28. *Procès* 2.143; *Le procès des Templiers d'Auvergne*, ed. Sève, p. 144.

29. *Procès* 2.13. See Forey, "Towards a Profile," pp. 196–204.

30. Jacques Hourlier, *L'Age Classique*, Histoire du droit et des institutions de l'église en Occident 10 (Saint-Amand-Montrond, 1974), pp. 161–62.

31. Hourlier, *L'Age Classique*, pp. 174–78.

32. Alan Forey, "Novitiate and Instruction in the Military Orders in the Twelfth and Thirteenth Centuries," *Speculum* 61 (1986), pp. 2–5. For justifications, see *Procès* 1.523, 528; 2.451.

33. Such as William of Santo Stefano, about whom more below; Andrew of Foggia, the Hospital's procurator in Rome and "advocate at the assizes of Tripoli" (*Cart Hosp* 2.479–80, 529, 596); and the Templar Gerald of Gaûche, who was "litteratus. . . . et in jure peritus" (*Procès* 1.379). See also Alan Forey, "Literacy and Learning in the Military Orders during the Twelfth and Thirteenth Centuries," *The Military Orders*, vol. 2, *Welfare and Warfare*, ed. Helen Nicholson (Aldershot, 1998), pp. 185–206; Vogel, *Das Recht*, p. 51.

34. Some in the Temple were never even instructed in the Rule; Jonathan Riley-Smith, "The Structures of the Orders of the Temple and the Hospital in c.1291," *Medieval Crusade*, ed. Susan Ridyard (Woodbridge, 2004), pp. 129–31.

35. Cristina Dondi, *The Liturgy of the Canons Regular of the Holy Sepulchre of Jerusalem* (Turnhout, 2004), pp. 41–42.

36. This explains why the Office in both Hospitaller and Templar houses was that of the Augustinian canons. Legras and Lemaître, "La pratique liturgique," pp. 80–89; Claverie, *L'Ordre du Temple en Terre Sainte* 1.333–40. The introduction of at least one eastern Christian element has been noticed with respect to the Templar liturgy; Cerrini, *La Révolution*, pp. 228–29. There does not seem to be enough evidence to justify Dr Cerrini's assertion (228) that the Hospitallers celebrated far fewer feasts than did the Templars.

37. For the Templars, see Claverie, *L'Ordre du Temple en Terre Sainte* 1.186–213.

38. *Cart Hosp* 3.46. For Malta, see Alain Blondy, *L'Ordre de Malte au XVIIIe siècle: Des dernières splendeurs à la ruine* (Paris, 2002), p. 71.

39. Riley-Smith, *The Knights of St John*, pp. 283–84.

40. See *Règle du Temple*, p. 145.

41. Riley-Smith, *The Knights of St John*, p. 348; Carraz, *L'ordre du Temple*, pp. 302–4.

42. It is, therefore, hard to draw a firm conclusion from the report that before the disaster at the Springs of Cresson in May 1187 the Templar convent consisted of at least ninety brothers. "L'Estoire de Eracles," *RHC Oc* 2.39.

43. William of Tyre, *Chronicon*, p. 554; Benjamin of Tudela, *Itinerary*, ed. and tr. Marcus Adler (London, 1907), p. 22. One hundred knights were summoned in ca. 1184 to a disciplinary convent to be held at La Fève; Marie-Luise Bulst-Thiele, *Sacrae Domus Militiae Templi Hierosolymitani Magistri* (Göttingen, 1974), p. 360.

44. Finke, *Papsttum* 2.352.

45. *Papsturkunden für Templer und Johanniter* 2.224. Benjamin of Tudela (*Itinerary*, p. 22) estimated four hundred, but he must have been confusing brothers-at-arms and hospital staff.

46. Kedar in "A Twelfth-Century Description," ed Kedar, p. 8. At least 900 patients were being cared for in late November 1177 when they were joined

by another 750 who had been wounded in the Battle of Montgisard. Roger of Moulins, "Letter," in Reinhold Röhricht, *Beiträge zur Geschichte der Kreuzzüge*, 2 vols (Berlin, 1874–78), 2.128.

47. *Cart Hosp* 1.425–29 (corrected in *Papsturkunden für Templer und Johanniter* 1.361); "Administrative Regulations," ed. Edgington, pp. 24–36; "A Twelfth-Century Description," ed. Kedar, pp. 18–26. For an early example of a volunteer, see Reginald of Durham, *Libellus de Vita et Miraculis S. Godrici, Heremite de Finchale*, Surtees Society 20 (London, 1847), p. 57.

48. Count Raymond of Toledo was staying in the Temple in Jerusalem in 1137; Rorgo Fretellus of Nazareth, *De locis sanctis terre Jerusalem*, ed. Petrus Boeren (Amsterdam, 1980), pp. 53–54. See also Benjamin of Tudela, *Itinerary*, p. 22; Vogel, *Das Recht*, p. 173.

49. Such as the apostolic and imperial notary Anthony Sicci and the so-called "Templar of Tyre," who was the grand master's lay secretary, in the later thirteenth century. *Procès* 1.641–48; The Templar of Tyre, *Cronaca*, pp. 128, 164, 168, 184, 204–6, 216–24. For Templar employees, see also Claverie, *L'Ordre du Temple en Terre Sainte* 1.216–19.

50. *Cart Hosp* 4.292.

51. Oliver of Paderborn, *Schriften*, ed. Hermann Hoogeweg (Tübingen, 1894), p. 255.

52. Pringle, *The Churches* 4.107; Eliezer Stern, "La commanderie de l'ordre des Hospitaliers à Acre," *Bulletin monumental* 164 (2006), pp. 56–57; Boas, *Archaeology of the Military Orders*, p. 55.

53. See Burgtorf, *The Central Convent*, p. 139, who may have underestimated the numbers.

54. Harper and Pringle, *Belmont*, p. 215.

55. *De constructione castri Saphet*, ed. Robert Huygens (Amsterdam, 1981), p. 41. See also Fidenzio of Padua, "Liber recuperationis," pp. 24–25.

56. *Procès* 2.138

57. Finke, *Papsttum* 2.342; *Procès* 2.259.

58. *Le procès des Templiers d'Auvergne*, ed. Sève, p. 251.

59. *Cart Hosp* 2.777.

60. *Cart Hosp* 2.778.

61. Willbrand of Oldenburg, "Itinerarium Terrae Sanctae," ed. Johann C. M. Laurent, *Peregrinatores medii aevi quatuor*, 2nd ed. (Leipzig, 1873), pp. 169–70. Guard duty at night was performed by twenty-eight sentries under the command of four brother knights.

62. See, for example, Barney Sloane and Gordon Malcolm, *Excavations at the Priory of the Order of the Hospital of St John of Jerusalem, Clerkenwell, London* (London, 2004), pp. 3–4, 199–203; Evelyn Lord, *The Knights Templar in Britain* (Harlow, 2004), pp. 33–49.

63. Riley-Smith, *The Knights of St John*, pp. 431, 460–61. This must have been the reason why the Templar castellan of Chastel Blanc and the Hospitaller castellans of Margat and Crac des Chevaliers had their own seals. *Cart Hosp* 2.603; William of Santo Stefano "Recueil," f. 298v. The seal of the castellan of Margat portrayed an elephant; that of the castellan of Crac des Chevaliers a castle.

64. See *Cart Hosp* 1.510. For the service of the vassals of Arsur, see *Cart Hosp* 3.6–7.

65. *Papsturkunden für Templer und Johanniter* 2.315–16; Willbrand of Oldenburg, "Itinerarium," p. 170; "Zwei unedierte Texte aus den Kreuzfahrerstaaten," ed. Hans Mayer, *Archiv für Diplomatik* 47/48 (2001/2002), p. 103; "Chartes d'Adam, abbé de Notre-Dame du Mont-Sion, concernant Gerard, éveque de Valanea, et le prieuré de Saint-Samson d'Orleans (1289)," ed. Alexandre Bruel, *ROL* 10 (1903–1904), pp. 7–15; *Cart Hosp* 1.144 (vidimus), 596; 2.169; Claude Cahen, *La Syrie du nord à l'époque des croisades et la principauté franque d'Antioche* (Paris, 1940), pp. 519–20; Riley-Smith, *The Knights of St John*, pp. 410–13.

66. See Riley-Smith, "Towards a History," p. 280.

67. Riley-Smith, *The Knights of St John*, pp. 249–50.

68. Anthony Luttrell, *The Town of Rhodes, 1306–1356* (Rhodes, 2003), p. 83; on Rhodes the individual *auberges* provided additional enclosed space.

69. Pringle, *The Churches* 1.12, 16–17. Cf. Boas, *Archaeology of the Military Orders*, p. 77. Small keeps such as those at Chastel Rouge and Tour Rouge, both of which were probably constructed before the orders took possession, and fragments of the Hospitaller grange or cell at Calansue, which had a *maison-forte*, are all that is left of buildings that may have housed smaller communities. Denys Pringle, *The Red Tower (al-Burj al-Ahmar): Settlement in the Plain of Sharon at the Time of the Crusaders and Mamluks AD 1099–1516* (London, 1986) pp. 16–18, 41–58, and passim.

70. *Cart Hosp* 1.271–72; Theoderic, "Peregrinatio," p. 189; Boas, *Archaeology of the Military Orders*, p. 229.

71. Pringle, *The Churches* 1.69–80; Oliver of Paderborn, *Schriften*, p. 171.

72. Harper and Pringle, *Belmont*, pp. 195–219. The scheme at Toron des Chevaliers may have been very similar; Boas, *Archaeology of the Military Orders*, pp. 255–56.

73. Boas, *Archaeology of the Military Orders*, pp. 229–30; Pringle, *The Churches* 1.95–101.

74. Paul Deschamps, *Les châteaux des croisés en Terre Sainte*, 3 vols (Paris, 1934–77), 3.249–58; Harper and Pringle, *Belmont*, pp. 211–12.

75. Boas, *Archaeology of the Military Orders*, pp. 251–52.

76. Deschamps, *Les châteaux* 1.105–305; 3.258, 272–85, 289–91.

77. Pringle, *The Churches* 2.323–28.

78. See Burgtorf, *The Central Convent*, pp. 80–81.

79. Pringle, *The Churches* 3.420–34.

80. Pringle, *The Churches* 3.192–207.

81. See Claverie, *L'Ordre du Temple en Terre Sainte* 1.242–9.

82. Pringle, *The Churches* 4.105–7; Stern, "La commanderie," pp. 53–59. See Jonathan Riley-Smith, "Guy of Lusignan, the Hospitallers and the Gates of Acre" *Dei gesta per Francos*, ed. Michel Balard, Benjamin Z. Kedar, and Jonathan Riley-Smith (Aldershot, 2001), pp. 111–15; Riley-Smith, "Further Thoughts," pp. 753–64.

83. Pringle, *The Churches* 4.94–100; Eliezer Stern, "The Church of St John in Acre," *Crusades* 4 (2005), p. 157; Stern, "La commanderie," p. 59.

84. Pringle, *The Churches* 4.101–2.

85. *Cart Hosp* 2.261. Riley-Smith, "Further Thoughts," pp. 763–64; Pringle, *The Churches* 4.114.

86. *Tabulae ordinis Theutonici*, ed. Ernst Strehlke (Berlin, 1869), p. 58; The Templar of Tyre, *Cronaca*, pp. 170, 222; Pringle, *The Churches* 4.115–16; Riley-Smith, *The Knights of St John*, p. 248. The site of this precursor of the *auberges* of the *langues* on Rhodes and Malta has been obliterated by the modern town.

87. *Cart Hosp* 2.36, 560; 3.226–28.

88. *Cart Hosp* 2.556.

89. *Cart Hosp* 2.544, 556; 3.227–28.

90. Oliver of Paderborn, *Schriften*, p. 171. See Rudolf Hiestand, "*Castrum Peregrinorum* e la fine del dominio crociato in Siria," *Acri 1291: La fine della presenza degli ordini militari in Terra Santa e i nuovi orientamenti nel XIV secolo*, ed. Francesco Tommasi (Perugia, 1996), p. 33.

91. Pringle, *The Churches* 4.19, 123, 156, 168–71.

92. See Hourlier, *L'Age Classique*, pp. 471–73. For the rights of the Temple and the Hospital to have priests, see Vogel, *Das Recht*, pp. 175–84; Riley-Smith, *The Knights of St John*, pp. 233–36, 377.

93. *Papsturkunden für Templer und Johanniter* 2.97.

94. *Papsturkunden für Templer und Johanniter* 2.99.

95. *Papsturkunden für Templer und Johanniter* 2.134.

96. Riley-Smith, *The Knights of St John*, p. 234.

97. Riley-Smith, *The Knights of St John*, pp. 234, 238.

98. Innocent III, *Register*, ed. Hageneder 1.823. See "Narratio de primordiis ordinis Theutonici," pp. 159–60.

99. Riley-Smith, *The Knights of St John*, pp. 338–39; Vogel, *Das Recht*, p. 176.

100. See *Règle du Temple*, pp. 235–36, 241, for the privileges enjoyed by Templar brother priests who were consecrated bishops. The military orders came to control the temporalities of the dioceses of Valenia, Tortosa, Sidon, and

perhaps whatever was left of the titular bishopric of Paneas. Rudolf Hiestand, "Templer- und Johanniterbistümer und -bischöfe im Heiligen Land," *Ritterorden und Kirche im Mittelalter,* ed. Zenon Hubert Nowak, Ordines Militares— Colloquia Torunensia 9 (Torun, 1997), pp. 143–61; Vogel, *Das Recht,* p. 182. The Templar Humbert, titular bishop of Paneas in 1272, was a bishop *in partibus infidelium;* Pierre Batiffol, Communication in "Correspondence," *Bulletin de la société nationale des antiquaires de France* (1891), p. 238, and Hiestand, "Templer- und Johanniterbistümer und -bischöfe," p. 153. So was William of St Jean, archbishop of Nazareth, whose *pallium* was brought out from Italy by one of his brothers in 1288; Nicholas IV, *Les Registres,* ed. Ernest Langlois (Paris, 1886–91), pp. 27–28. See Hiestand, "Templer- und Johanniterbistümer und -bischöfe," pp. 153–54; Bernard Hamilton, *The Latin Church in the Crusader States: The Secular Church* (London, 1980), p. 279; Claverie, *L'Ordre du Temple en Terre Sainte* 2.168–71. For Valenia and the bishop's residence in Margat, see above, note 65. For Tortosa, see Hiestand, "Templer- und Johanniterbistümer und -bischöfe," pp. 148–51.

101. Burgtorf, *The Central Convent,* pp. 329–38.

102. For Templar conventual priors, see *Procès* 1.646; Burgtorf, *The Central Convent,* pp. 336–38; Vogel, *Das Recht,* pp. 177–78. For Hospitaller ones, *Cart Hosp* 1.121–22, 222–23, 272–73, 276–79, 300–301, 306–8, 323–24, 415–16, 479–80, 583, 595–96; 2.78–79, 553, 673–75; 3.61; Burgtorf, *The Central Convent,* pp. 329–36. The chief priests in each community were also called priors. For a Templar prior in Tripoli, see Louis de Mas Latrie, *Histoire de l'île de Chypre sous le règne des princes de la maison de Lusignan,* 3 vols (Paris, 1852–61), 3.664. For Hospitaller priors at Acre, when it was still a commandery (*Cart Hosp* 1.323–24, 445, 480), Crac des Chevaliers (*Cart Hosp* 2.662), Margat (*Cart Hosp* 2.477), and Mont Pèlerin (*Cart Hosp* 1.72, 118; *Cartulaire du Saint-Sépulcre,* p. 189).

103. *Procès* 1.646. Burgtorf (*The Central Convent,* pp. 452–3) has made the unlikely suggestion that senior Templars were being polite to a man who was "physically challenged."

104. James of Vitry, "Sermo XXXVII," p. 412.

105. *Cart Hosp* 1.346. See Legras and Lemaître, "La pratique liturgique," pp. 95–96.

106. In 1254 a church council in Palestine legislated against cases of corruption among the secular clergy in Acre; *The Synodicum Nicosiense and other Documents of the Latin Church of Cyprus, 1196–1373,* ed. Christopher Schabel (Nicosia, 2001), pp. 174–76.

107. *Procès* 1.646–47.

108. Riley-Smith, *The Knights of St John,* pp. 390–420. For a case relating to the Templars on Cyprus, see Pierre-Vincent Claverie, "L'ordre du Temple au coeur d'une crise politique majeure: La *Querela Cypri* des années 1279–1285," *Le moyen âge* 104 (1998), p. 498. For the general picture, see Hourlier, *L'Age Classique,* pp. 457–68.

109. *Cart Hosp* 1.345–47, 425; 3.77; Riley-Smith, *The Knights of St John*, p. 235. One priest was attached to the hospital, another to the infirmary for sick brothers, and a third to the mortuary chapel in the order's cemetery.

110. *Cart Hosp* 1.346.

111. See *Cart Hosp* 1.326.

112. *Cart Hosp* 1.435.

113. "Le Comté de Tripoli dans les chartes du fonds des Porcellet," ed. Jean Richard, *Bibliothèque de l'Ecole des Chartes* 130 (1972), pp. 371–73.

114. Jonathan Riley-Smith, "Were the Templars Guilty?" *Medieval Crusade*, ed. Susan Ridyard (Woodbridge, 2004), p. 112.

115. The two friars stationed there were martyred with the rest of the garrison. Fidenzio of Padua, "Liber recuperationis," pp. 24–25; *Biblioteca Bio-Bibliografica della Terra Santa*, comp. Gulobovich, 1.260–61, 264.

116. *Le procès des Templiers d'Auvergne*, ed. Sève, p. 119; also see pp. 114, 126, 132, 137, 143, 149, 154, 156, 188, 201, 215, 217, 219, 222, 224, 225, 227, 231, 232, 238, 242; *The Trial of the Templars in the Papal State*, pp. 195, 257; Schottmüller, *Der Untergang* 2.255, 258, 287, 290, 317, 396–98.

117. See Elm, *Umbilicus Mundi*, pp. 498–506; Vogel, *Das Recht*, pp. 229–33.

118. Riley-Smith, *The Knights of St John*, p. 238.

119. *Cart Hosp* 3.46; *Règle du Temple*, pp. 304–5. A candidate for reception in the Temple had to be already knighted, and young boys would be dubbed just before reception. *Règle de Temple*, pp. 234, 241. See *Procès* 1.417, 454; "Inquesta," ed. Frale, p. 200. But the orders could dub men knights if they so wished. See *Cart Hosp* 2.40.

120. *Procès* 2.13, 116, 265–66.

121. Schottmüller, *Der Untergang* 2.46. Was he of illegitimate birth? See *Règle du Temple*, pp. 194, 234.

122. *Procès* 2.132.

123. Carraz, *L'ordre du Temple*, p. 297.

124. For sergeants who were literate or knew Latin, *Procès* 1.254, 474, 538, 560, 600; 2.111, 227, 236, 256, 261, 267; *Conciliae Magni Britannie* 2.334.

125. As commander of the *palais*, the main building of the conventual compound (*Règle du Temple*, pp. 175, 178, 193, 315), or as commanders of the vault (or warehouses), shipyard and cattle-yards in Acre (*Règle du Temple*, pp. 99, 307, 314–15), or as casaliers, who were responsible for the supervision of villages in the countryside (*Cart Hosp* 2.885; The Templar of Tyre, *Cronaca*, p. 110; "L'Estoire de Eracles" 2.455).

126. Innocent III, "Register," *PL* 216.975; *Cart Hosp* 3.58; Finke, *Papsttum* 2.371.

127. *Règle du Temple*, p. 312.

128. *Règle du Temple*, pp. 297, 312–13. For another smith, see Schottmüller, *Der Untergang* 2.368.

129. *Règle du Temple*, pp. 290–91.

130. *Cart Hosp* 2.548.

131. One casalier was referred to by that title (*Cart Hosp* 3.314) and another seems to have had the title of *ra'is* (*Cart Hosp* 1.84), the office usually held by someone who mediated between the settlers and the indigenous, which probably meant that he was a casalier as well. See Jonathan Riley-Smith, *The Feudal Nobility and the Kingdom of Jerusalem, 1174–1277* (London, 1973), pp. 47–49. Sergeants were also to be found as petty commander (*Cart Hosp* 2.494), commander of the vault and seneschal of the *palais* in Jerusalem and Acre (*Cart Hosp* 1.113–15, 136, 226), brother of the *parmentarie*, the clothes store and tailoring department (Riley-Smith, *The Knights of St John*, pp. 313, 338), *custos* of the *Asnerie* just outside Jerusalem, where pack-animals were stabled (*Cart Hosp* 1.349, 416, 503), *auberger*, presumably a janitor in the *auberge* in Acre (*Cart Hosp* 2.565), and master of works (*Cart Hosp*, 1.350; 2.262). Or they had military functions, such as arbalester (*Cart Hosp* 1.480) and master esquire of the convent (*Cart Hosp* 2.675).

132. *Cart Hosp* 2.494, 536, 675.

133. *Cart Hosp* 1.150, 157.

134. See Riley-Smith, *The Knights of St John*, pp. 239–40; Alan Forey, *The Templars in the Corona de Aragón*, pp. 280–81; Jonathan Riley-Smith, "The Roles of Hospitaller and Templar Sergeants," forthcoming.

135. Pietro Scarpellini, "La chiesa de San Bevignate, i Templari e la pittura perugina del Duecento," *Templari e Ospitalieri in Italia: La chiesa di San Bevignate in Perugia*, ed. Mario Roncetti, Pietro Scarpellini and Francesco Tommasi (Milan, 1987), pp. 128–29.

136. *Die ursprüngliche Templerregel*, pp. 140–41; William of Tyre, *Chronicon*, p. 554; *Règle du Temple*, pp. 235–36, 241, 304–5.

137. *Règle du Temple*, pp. 235–36, 241.

138. Nicholson, *Templars, Hospitallers and Teutonic Knights*, pp. 25–26.

139. Riley-Smith, *The Knights of St John*, pp. 238–39. See William of Santo Stefano, "Recueil," f. 143v.

140. *Cart Hosp* 1.63–64, 68. The only injunctions in the Rule were to dress humbly, never to wear expensive furs or fabrics, and to display crosses on their clothes; Riley-Smith, *The Knights of St John*, p. 254. For the Cassinese Benedictines at St Mary of the Latins, see "Papst- Kaiser- und Normannenurkunden aus Unteritalien," ed. Walther Holtzmann, *QFIAB* 35 (1955), p. 51.

141. *Cart Hosp* 4.120. Even as late as the fifteenth century the illustrator of the manuscript of William Caoursin's *Obsidionis Rhodiae urbis descriptio* (1480), who generally portrayed the brothers in black or red, depicted some members of the grand master's council in brown over-coats; Paris, Bibliothèque Nationale Ms. Lat. 6067, fol. 83v.

142. *Procès* 1.545; 2.95. See *Règle du Temple*, p. 249.

143. See Schottmüller, *Der Untergang* 2.132. A knight even appears to have been in the service of a very senior sergeant-commander in France; *Procès* 2.235.

144. *Procès* 2.137. See also Vogel, *Das Recht*, pp. 171–73, 188–89.

145. Anthony Luttrell and Helen Nicholson, *Hospitaller Women in the Middle Ages* (Aldershot, 2006), passim, esp. Myra Struckmeyer, "The Sisters of the Order of Saint John at Mynchin Buckland," p. 89.

146. See *Cart Hosp* 1.115–16.

147. Riley-Smith, *The Knights of St John*, pp. 240–42.

148. "A Twelfth-Century Description," ed. Kedar, pp. 24–25.

149. *Cart Hosp* 2.261.

150. Riley-Smith, *The Knights of St John*, pp. 401–3.

151. *Cart Hosp* 3.48. Known from its confirmation in 1262.

152. See Alan Forey, "Women and the Military Orders in the Twelfth and Thirteenth Centuries," repr. in *Hospitaller Women in the Middle Ages*, ed. Anthony Luttrell and Helen Nicholson (Aldershot, 2006), pp. 43–69.

153. See Cerrini, *La Révolution*, pp. 180–83; Helen Nicholson, "Women in Templar and Hospitaller Commanderies," *La Commanderie, Institution des ordres militaires dans l'Occident médiéval*, ed. Anthony Luttrell and Léon Pressouyre (Paris, 2002), pp. 125–34.

Three   GOVERNANCE

1. "Annales monasterii Burtonensis," p. 494; *Monumentorum Boicorum* 29 ii, p. 201.

2. *Cart Hosp* 4.291–93.

3. A good, although occasionally overenthusiastic, account of their twelfth-century possessions is to be found in Claverie, "Les débuts," pp. 557–69. They included Gaza (Pringle, *The Churches* 1.208–20), Toron des Chevaliers (Pringle, *The Churches* 2.5–9; Adrian Boas, "Latrun," *Crusades* 4 [2005], pp. 159–60; Boas, *Archaeology of the Military Orders*, pp. 255–56), Chastel Hernault (Pringle, *Secular Buildings*, pp. 106–7), Destroit (Pringle, *Secular Buildings*, p. 47), Maldoim (or Cisterna Rubea) (Pringle, *Secular Buildings*, pp. 78–79), Casel des Plains (Pringle, *Secular Buildings*, p. 108), Quarantaine (Pringle, *Secular Buildings*, p. 52), Vadum Jacob (Ronnie Ellenblum, *Crusader Castles and Modern Histories* [Cambridge, 2007], pp. 258–74), and La Fève (Pringle, *Secular Buildings*, p. 49). It is not clear whether a commandery in southern Galilee, called by the Templars "Caco," but obviously not the settlement in the lordship of Caesarea, was still in the order's hands in the thirteenth century; Pringle, *The Red Tower*, p. 60. In 1148 the Templars had abandoned a march in the southwest of the county of Edessa; Claverie, "Les débuts," p. 577.

4. Boas, *Archaeology of the Military Orders*, p. 233.

5. Pringle, *The Churches* 1.69–80; Claverie, *L'Ordre du Temple en Terre Sainte* 1.259–71. Nearby was Merle (Boas, *Archaeology of the Military Orders*, p. 247) and Cafarlet, which was bought from the Hospitallers in 1255 and lost in 1265 (Boas, *Archaeology of the Military Orders*, pp. 231–32).

6. Pringle, *The Churches* 2.206–9; Hervé Barbé and Emanuel Damati, "La forteresse médiévale de Safed: Données récentes de l'archéologie," *Crusades* 3 (2004), pp. 171–78; Claverie, *L'Ordre du Temple en Terre Sainte* 1.273–81.

7. Reinhold Röhricht, Communication in "Chronique," *ROL* 6 (1898), pp. 333–34. See Pringle, *The Churches* 2.317–29; Deschamps, *Les châteaux* 2.224–33; Claverie, *L'Ordre du Temple en Terre Sainte* 1.282–90. The lordship comprised the city and its territories as well as two large castles. For Beaufort, see Deschamps, *Les châteaux* 2.177–208; Pringle, *The Churches* 1.110; Pringle, *Secular Buildings*, p. 31; Claverie, *L'Ordre du Temple en Terre Sainte* 1.289–90.

8. Deschamps, *Les châteaux* 3.249–58; Claverie, *L'Ordre du Temple en Terre Sainte* 1.295–96.

9. Deschamps, *Les châteaux* 3.313–16.

10. Deschamps, *Les châteaux* 3.287–92; Claverie, *L'Ordre du Temple en Terre Sainte* 1.297–306. For its acquisition, see "The Templars and the castle of Tortosa," pp. 284–88.

11. Robert W. Edwards, "Bağras and Armenian Cilicia: A Reassessment," *Revue des études arméniennes* ns 17 (1983), pp. 415–68.

12. Robert Edwards, *The Fortifications of Armenian Cilicia* (Washington DC, 1987), p. 253; Deschamps, *Les châteaux* 3.361; Claverie, *L'Ordre du Temple en Terre Sainte* 1.309–12.

13. The Templar of Tyre, *Cronaca*, p. 124; "L'Estoire de Eracles" 2.457; Innocent III, "Register," *PL* 216.430.

14. Identified as Çalan by Edwards, *The Fortifications*, pp. 99–102. Cf. Deschamps, *Les châteaux* 3.363–65; Claverie, *L'Ordre du Temple en Terre Sainte* 1.309.

15. Deschamps's identification of Roche Guillaume (*Les châteaux* 3.363–65) was accepted by Claverie (*L'Ordre du Temple en Terre Sainte* 1.312–15; 2.414), but had already been demolished by Edwards (*The Fortifications*, p. 99).

16. For the march, see Jonathan Riley-Smith, "The Templars and the Teutonic Knights in Cilician Armenia," *The Cilician Kingdom of Armenia*, ed. Thomas Boase (Edinburgh, 1978), pp. 92–117. Before 1186, and perhaps for some time afterwards, the Templars had a castle in the south of the principality of Antioch called Brahim, but this eventually passed to the Hospitallers with the rest of the environs of Margat. *Règle du Temple*, p. 313; *Les Archives*, ed. Delaville Le Roulx, pp. 134–35; Cahen, *La Syrie du nord*, p. 176.

17. See especially *The Catalan Rule*, pp. 80–86.

18. Schottmüller, *Der Untergang* 2.206; *Conciliae Magni Britannie* 2.366; *The Catalan Rule*, pp. 80–84; The Templar of Tyre, *Cronaca*, p. 282.

19. Deschamps, *Les châteaux* 1, passim. It has been argued that the twelfth-century elements date from a rebuilding after the earthquake of 1170; Thomas Biller, "Der Crac des Chevaliers—Neue Forschungen," *Château Gaillard* 20 (2002), pp. 51–55. For the date of the gift of Crac des Chevaliers the Hospitallers—1142 or 1144—see Jean Richard, "*Cum omni raisagio montanee* . . . propos de la cession du Crac des Chevaliers aux Hospitaliers," *Itinéraires d'Orient*, ed. Raoul Curiel and Rika Gyselen (Bures-sur-Yvette, 1994), p. 187. In the county of Tripoli the Hospitallers also held Chastel Rouge (Pringle, *The Red Tower*, pp. 16–18) and perhaps Coliath (Boas, *Archaeology of the Military Orders*, p. 238).

20. Deschamps, *Les châteaux* 3.259–85. Margat had precedence over Crac in William of Santo Stefano's list of officers; William of Santo Stefano, "Recueil," f. 298v.

21. Riley-Smith, *The Knights of St John*, p. 132. Edwards (*The Fortifications*, pp. 221–29) concludes that Camardesium is of Frankish, in other words Hospitaller, construction throughout.

22. Pringle, *The Churches* 1.95–101.

23. With its important dependent commandery at Fons Emaus and infirmary at Aqua Bella. Harper and Pringle, *Belmont*, passim; Pringle, *The Churches* 1.7–17, 239–50.

24. Pringle, *The Churches* 1.120–22. Other smaller twelfth-century castles, which were not reoccupied, were Calcalia, which was important enough to be included in a list of places lost to Saladin in 1187 (*Cart Hosp* 1.412, 445, 480; "Zwei unbekannte Hilfersuchen des Patriarchen Eraclius vor den Fall Jerusalem (1187)," ed. Nikolas Jaspert, *Deutsches Archiv* 60 [2004], p. 514) and possibly St Job (Pringle, *The Churches* 1.106–7).

25. Ellenblum, *Crusader Castles*, pp. 261–74.

26. *De constructione castri Saphet*, p. 41.

27. Riley-Smith, "The Crown of France and Acre," p. 48.

28. *Procès* 1.646. For Templar mercenaries, see also Claverie, *L'Ordre du Temple en Terre Sainte* 1.220–25.

29. Willbrand of Oldenburg, "Itinerarium," p. 170.

30. *De constructione castri Saphet*, p. 41.

31. *The Catalan Rule*, pp. 80–86. See Judith Upton-Ward, "The Surrender of Gaston and the Rule of the Templars," *The Military Orders: Fighting for the Faith and Caring for the Sick*, ed. Malcolm Barber (Aldershot, 1994), pp. 179–88.

32. Manueth (Boas, *Archaeology of the Military Orders*, p. 246) and the Tor de l'Ospital (Pringle, *Secular Buildings*, p. 41).

33. *Cart Hosp* 2.777, 815–17, 881–83.

34. Riley-Smith, *The Knights of St John*, p. 133.

35. Riley-Smith, *The Knights of St John*, pp. 133–34; Israel Roll and Benjamin Arubas, "Le château d'Arsur," *Bulletin monumental* 164 (2006), pp. 67–79, esp. pp. 77–78.

36. Matthew Paris, *Chronica maiora* 4.291.

37. They had several minor infirmaries outside the headquarters, for example in Acre and Nablus in the twelfth century. *Cart Hosp* 1.323–24; "Zwei unbekannte Diplome der lateinischen Könige von Jerusalem aus Lucca," ed. Rudolf Hiestand, *QFIAB*, 50 (1971), p. 54.

38. "Cooked in water" could also mean poached, of course.

39. "Administrative Regulations," ed. Edgington, pp. 24–36; "A Twelfth-Century Description," ed Kedar, pp. 19–24; *Cart Hosp* 1.425–29.

40. *De constructione castri Saphet*, p. 41.

41. Templar rule over Cyprus had lasted for less than a year after the order bought it in 1191 from Richard I of England, but the brothers had quite extensive estates on the island thereafter, and the land commander in Limassol was responsible for convents, besides his own, in the castle of Gastria and in houses in Nicosia, Paphos, and Famagusta. See Claverie, *L'Ordre du Temple en Terre Sainte* 1.315–19; also Peter Edbury, *The Kingdom of Cyprus and the Crusades, 1191–1374* (Cambridge, 1991), pp. 77–78; Nicholas Coureas, *The Latin Church in Cyprus, 1195–1312* (Aldershot, 1997), pp. 121–55. The Hospitaller estates, gathered at this stage into a single commandery at Limassol, were concentrated in the south of the island and there were convents in Nicosia and Limassol and in the small castle of Kolossi nearby; Riley-Smith, *The Knights of St John*, pp. 311, 428, 430, 432, 443, 447.

42. In the 1170s the Hospitallers commissioned Greek artists to paint frescoes, tailored to Latin requirements, in the church at Fons Emaus; Folda, *The Art of the Crusaders*, pp. 382–90. After 1187 local Christian artists redecorated the chapel at Margat and after 1202 the chapel at Crac des Chevaliers; Jaroslav Folda, *Crusader Art in the Holy Land from the Third Crusade to the Fall of Acre, 1187–1291* (Cambridge, 2005), pp. 32–34, 78, 97–99.

43. Pringle, *The Churches* 3.417–34.

44. Anthony Luttrell, "Préface" to *Les Légendes de l'Hôpital de Saint-Jean de Jérusalem*, ed. Antoine Calvet (Paris, 2000), pp. 10–11.

45. Dondi, *The Liturgy*, p. 171.

46. Pringle, *The Churches* 1.7–17.

47. Pringle, *The Churches* 2.333; Boas, *Archaeology of the Military Orders*, p. 87; Claverie, *L'Ordre du Temple en Terre Sainte* 1.256.

48. Camille Enlart, *Les monuments des croisés dans le royaume de Jérusalem: architecture religieuse et civile*, 2 vols and 2 albums (Paris, 1925–28), 2.395–430. For an example of the Templars' relations with the church at Tortosa, see *Procès* 1.645.

49. "Pelrinages et pardouns de Acre," ed. Henri Michelant and Gaston Raynaud, *Itinéraires à Jérusalem et descriptions de la Terre Sainte rédigés en français* (Geneva, 1882), p. 235.

50. The Templars had Port Bonnel and Calamella, and the Hospitallers had Valenia in the principality of Antioch. In the kingdom of Jerusalem the Templars had Chastel Pèlerin and Sidon, and the Hospitallers had held Bethgibelin in the twelfth century and briefly occupied Arsur and Ascalon in the thirteenth.

51. For a case relating to competing jurisdictions and involving the Teutonic Knights, see *Tabulae ordinis Theutonici*, pp. 85–87.

52. *Cart Hosp* 1.21, 172; 2.780.

53. *Cart Hosp* 1.134, 140.

54. Mas Latrie, *Histoire de l'île de Chypre* 3.666.

55. Pringle, *The Churches* 2.332–33; Boas, *Archaeology of the Military Orders*, p. 88.

56. *Cart Hosp* 1.315.

57. *Cart Hosp* 1.75, 77, 87–88, 171–73, 315, 446–47, 683; 2.483, 486–87, 489, 780; 3.35, 59–60, 238. See Riley-Smith, *The Knights of St John*, p. 446; Claverie, *L'Ordre du Temple en Terre Sainte* 1.250–53.

58. See *De constructione castri Saphet*, p. 41.

59. For the Templars: *Documenti sulle relazioni delle città toscane coll'Oriente cristiano e coi Turchi fino all'anno 1531*, ed. Giuseppe Müller, Documenti degli archivi toscani 3 (Florence, 1879), pp. 27; *Cart Hosp* 1.527; *Le procès des Templiers d'Auvergne*, ed. Sève, p. 251; *Conciliae Magni Britannie* 2.337; *Règle du Temple*, pp. 289, 314, 326; Bulst-Thiele, *Sacrae Domus*, p. 360. For the Hospitallers: *Cart Hosp* 1.132, 145, 617; 2.875–76; *Documenti sulle relazioni*, p. 27. The commander of Tyre still ranked as a capitular bailiff after 1291; see William of Santo Stefano, "Recueil," f. 299v.

60. For the Templar grand commander: *Règle du Temple*, pp. 80, 102, 278, 318–19, 339; *Cart Hosp* 2.859–63; 3.254; Mas Latrie, *Histoire de l'île de Chypre* 3.665–66. For references to the Templar house in Tripoli, see *Conciliae Magni Britannie* 2.373; *Tabulae ordinis Theutonici*, p. 35; The Templar of Tyre, *Cronaca*, pp. 146, 156; "L'Estoire de Eracles" 2.468–69, 481; *Règle du Temple*, pp. 289, 294; *Bullarium Franciscanum, Romanorum Pontificum Constitutiones, Epistolas, ac Diplomata*, ed. Giovanni Giacinto Sbaralea et al., 7 vols (Rome, 1758–1904) 3.327. See Claverie, *L'Ordre du Temple en Terre Sainte* 1.291. For the Hospitallers: *Cart Hosp* 1.649; 2.43, 185, 505, 596, 755, 877; 3.61.

61. For the Templar grand commander: *Règle du Temple*, pp. 80, 102–3, 278; William of Tyre, *Chronicon*, p. 874; Matthew Paris, *Chronica maiora* 3.405; Amedée Trudon des Ormes, "Etude sur les possessions de l'ordre de Temple," *Mémoires de la société des antiquaires de Picardie* 32 (1894), pp. 367–68; *Documenti inediti reguardanti le due crociate di San Ludovico IX re di Francia*, ed. Luigi

Belgrano (Genoa, 1859), p. 60; *Cart Hosp* 2.859–63, 885; *The Catalan Rule*, pp. 80–82. See also "Annales de Terre Sainte," ed. Reinhold Röhricht and Gaston Raynaud, *AOL* 2 (1884), p. 435; *Règle du Temple*, pp. 289, 304, 326, 339. After the loss of Antioch the Templar office was renamed the grand commandery of Armenia. *Cart Hosp* 2.859–63; Schottmüller, *Der Untergang* 2.206. See *Règle du Temple*, p. 339; Vogel, *Das Recht*, pp. 242–43. For the Hospitallers: "Ein unbekanntes Privileg Fürst Bohemonds II für das Hospital," ed. Rudolf Hiestand, *Archiv für Diplomatik* 43 (1997), p. 45; *Cart Hosp* 1.177, 326, 440, 446–47, 574–75, 649; 2.190, 345, 675; *Codice diplomatico*, ed. Paoli 1.258; Trudon des Ormes, "Etude," pp. 367–68.

   62. For Tripoli and Antioch, see *Procès* 1.645; 2.16, 147; Mas Latrie, *Histoire de l'île de Chypre* 3.665–66; *Règle du Temple*, pp. 326, 329; Finke, *Papsttum* 2.371; *Cart Hosp* 3.254. On the thirteenth-century mainland the Templars still had communities living in Beirut (*Règle du Temple*, pp. 224, 295), Caesarea (*Règle du Temple*, p. 304), Gibelet (Mas Latrie, *Histoire de l'île de Chypre* 3.665) and perhaps Somelaria (Pringle, *The Churches* 2.332–33; Boas, *Archaeology of the Military Orders*, pp. 87–88). There was possibly another commandery at Arsur for a time; *Règle du Temple*, p. 308. The Templars appear to have lost Tiberias (*Cart Hosp* 1.241; *Tabulae ordinis Theutonici*, p. 6) and perhaps Jaffa (*Règle du Temple*, pp. 316–17). Financial need may have led the Hospitallers to merge the centers of a few of their commanderies: Laodicea-Gibel (*Cart Hosp* 1.436–37) with Margat; Mont Pèlerin (*Cart Hosp* 1.72, 118, 421; *Cartulaire du chapitre du Saint-Sépulcre*, p. 189) with Tripoli (*Cart Hosp* 1.649; 2.43, 185, 505, 596, 755, 877; 3.61); and Spina (*Cart Hosp* 1.199, 245, 496) with Jaffa (*Cart Hosp* 1.71, 73, 145; 2.64–65, 575). A community at Beirut presumably survived (*Cart Hosp* 1.88), together with one in the tiny castle of Chastel Rouge, north of Tripoli (Deschamps, *Les châteaux* 3.317–19; Pringle, *The Red Tower*, pp. 16–18). A new commandery was established in Cilician Armenia in 1248 to look after the order's properties there (*Cart Hosp* 2.675). In the twelfth century there had been brothers living at Calansue, where there still survives the remains of a twelfth-century hall (*Cart Hosp* 1.84, 97; Pringle, *The Red Tower*, pp. 41–58), at Cacho (although the order did not own the whole estate; see Pringle, *The Red Tower*, pp. 59–60) and in a commandery at Tiberias (*Cart Hosp* 1.71, 73, 272, 427). Tricaria, to the east of the principality of Antioch (*Cart Hosp* 1.326) and Turbessel, far to the north in the county of Edessa (*Cart Hosp* 1.89–90; Cahen, *La Syrie du nord*, pp. 514, 526) had been lost earlier in the twelfth century.

   63. *The Catalan Rule*, pp. 80–86.

   64. *Cart Hosp* 2.596, 603; *Règle du Temple*, pp. 290–91.

   65. *Procès* 1.645; 2.144, 153, 222; *Le procès des Templiers d'Auvergne*, ed. Sève, pp. 146, 220; *Les Archives*, ed. Delaville Le Roulx, pp. 112–13; *Codice diplomatico*, ed. Paoli 1.250; *Cart Hosp* 2.603; Mas Latrie, *Histoire de l'île de Chypre*

3.665; *Règle du Temple*, p. 306; Finke, *Papsttum* 2.371. See also *Early Mamluk Diplomacy (1260–1290): Treaties of Baybars and Qalawun with Christian Rulers*, trans. Peter M. Holt (Leiden, 1995), pp. 66–68.

66. *Procès* 1.645; 2.138; *Le procès des Templiers d'Auvergne*, ed. Sève, p. 186; *Cart Hosp* 3.31, 33.

67. *Règle du Temple*, pp. 312, 326; *Cart Hosp* 3.31, 33. For the convent, lesser officials, and individual brothers at Saphet, see *De constructione castri Saphet*, pp. 41; The Templar of Tyre, *Cronaca*, pp. 84, 110; "L'Estoire de Eracles" 2.455; *Règle du Temple*, pp. 297, 312–13.

68. *Cart Hosp* 3.31, 33; *Procès* 2.238–39; Schottmüller, *Der Untergang* 2.79; *Conciliae Magni Britannie* 2.345, 358; *Règle du Temple*, p. 326; The Templar of Tyre, *Cronaca*, p. 84. Chastel Pèlerin had a prison, where three brothers convicted in a notorious case of sodomy were imprisoned during the mastership of Thomas Berard; *Règle du Temple*, pp. 290, 297–98, 309, 312; *Procès* 1.386–87; 2.223; "Inquesta," ed. Frale, pp. 200, 208.

69. *Cart Hosp* 1.116–18, 281–82, 400, 445, 480, 493–94; 2.43, 185, 603, 675. For a subordinate officer, see *Cart Hosp* 3.322.

70. *Cart Hosp* 1.491–96, 596, 648–49, 683; 2.56, 71, 675. For subordinate officers, see *Cart Hosp* 2.477.

71. The ruins of three mills can still be seen near Acre. At one of these sites, Manueth, the evidence of sugar production is very well preserved; Boas, *Archaeology of the Military Orders*, pp. 240–41, 246, 250. For examples of agreements on, and the sharing of, water for irrigation, see *Cart Hosp* 3.239; "Le Comté de Tripoli dans les chartes du fonds des Porcellet," pp. 374–77.

72. Stern, "La commanderie," p. 56; Edna Stern, "The Hospitaller Order in Acre and Manueth: The Ceramic Evidence," *The Military Orders*, vol 3, *History and Heritage*, ed. Victor Mallia-Milanes (Aldershot, 2008), pp. 207–8. See also Boas, *Archaeology of the Military Orders*, p. 93.

73. *Cart Hosp* 2.382–83, 531.

74. Emmanuel G. Rey, *Recherches géographiques et historiques sur la domination des Latins en Orient* (Paris, 1877), pp. 38–39. See Riley-Smith, *The Feudal Nobility*, p. 46. The Hospitaller commanderies on Mont Pèlerin near Tripoli and in Tiberias were also committed to sugar production; *Cart Hosp* 1.427. The commandery in Antioch provided the hospital with cotton; *Cart Hosp* 1.427.

75. Bronstein, *The Hospitallers*, pp. 52–56.

76. The Hospital established perhaps three (Bethgibelin, Fons Emaus, and possibly Cabor) and acquired three others (Ste Marie, Casale Album, and Manueth). Ronnie Ellenblum, *Frankish Rural Settlement in the Latin Kingdom of Jerusalem* (Cambridge, 1998), pp. 117, 128–35, 142–43, 154, 176–77, 198–204. There also appears to have been one at Calansue, but this answered not to the order but to the lord of Caesarea; Pringle, *The Red Tower*, pp. 14–15. The Temple

founded at least two (Chastel Pèlerin and Saffran); Pringle, *The Churches* 1.70, 75–80; Ellenblum, *Frankish Rural Settlement*, pp. 143–44.

77. "Administrative Regulations," ed. Edgington, p. 26; *Cart Hosp* 1.340. See also Harper and Pringle, *Belmont*, p. 218; Ellenblum, *Frankish Rural Settlement*, pp. 128–31.

78. This was Chola; see Hans Mayer, *Die Kanzlei der lateinischen Könige von Jerusalem*, 2 vols (Hanover, 1996), 2.899. Until recently the remains of a warehouse and neighboring tower could be seen, suggesting an agricultural centre. See Pringle, *The Red Tower*, pp. 21–22.

79. *Cart Hosp* 2.529.

80. *Cart Hosp* 2.382–83, 531.

81. See Burgtorf, *The Central Convent*, passim.

82. For the Temple, see *Règle du Temple*, pp. 80, 142–52; Claverie, *L'Ordre du Temple en Terre Sainte* 1.145–57.

83. For the Temple, Everard of Barres, Arnald of Torroja, Gilbert Erail, possibly Peter of Montaigu, Armand of Peragors, William of Sonnac and William of Beaujeu, although the previous careers of two, Philip of Plessis and William of Chartres, are unknown and one of those chosen from among the brothers already serving in the convent, Renaud of Vichier, had been grand commander of France until two years before his election. Bulst-Thiele, *Sacrae Domus*, passim. For the Hospital, Garnier of Nablus, Geoffrey of Donjon, Alfonso of Portugal, Guérin, Bertrand of Comps, John of Villiers and William of Villaret. The previous career of Bertrand of Thessy is unknown. Riley-Smith, *The Knights of St John*, passim.

84. Burgtorf, *The Central Convent*, p. 96.

85. *De constructione castri Saphet*, pp. 37–38. But perhaps also *Règle du Temple*, pp. 287–88.

86. Vogel, *Das Recht*, pp. 147, 255–60, 311–21; Burgtorf, *The Central Convent*, passim; Riley-Smith, *The Knights of St John*, pp. 279–86.

87. Riley-Smith, *The Knights of St John*, pp. 292–96.

88. William's kinship with the Capetians was recognized within his order (The Templar of Tyre, *Cronaca*, p. 142) and by Charles of Anjou, to whom he was a "carissimus consanguineus" (*I registri della cancelleria angioina*, ed. Riccardo Filangieri et al., 30 vols [Naples, 1950–71] 26.207).

89. Riley-Smith, "The Crown of France and Acre," pp. 54–56.

90. The Templar of Tyre, *Cronaca*, pp. 194, 202. One is tempted to believe that this was Qala'un's son and designated successor Salah ad-Din Khalil, known in history as al-Ashraf, who was himself to seize Acre in 1291 and transmitted to William an announcement of his final advance on the city; The Templar of Tyre, *Cronaca*, pp. 204–6. For William's treaty with Qala'un of 1282, see *Early Mamluk Diplomacy*, pp. 66–68.

91. *Procès* 1.645; 2.209. See Burgtorf, *The Central Convent*, pp. 593–95.

92. *Procès* 1.44–45. See also *Procès* 1.187; 2.209, 214–15.

93. *Procès* 2.222. See also Riley-Smith, "The Structures," p. 140.

94. See Hourlier, *L'Age classique*, pp. 377–92.

95. *Règle du Temple*, pp. 80–81, 83, 294, 297, 318, 326; *The Catalan Rule*, p. 56.

96. Prutz, *Entwicklung*, pp. 289–91 (also ed. in Claverie, *L'Ordre du Temple en Terre Sainte* 2.427–28); "Dei Tempieri e del loro processo in Toscana," pp. 452–55; The Templar of Tyre, *Cronaca*, p. 84; Bulst-Thiele, *Sacrae Domus*, pp. 242–45. See "L'Estoire de Eracles" 2.445; "Annales de Terre Sainte," pp. 449–50; also Vogel, *Das Recht*, pp. 54–55; Burgtorf, *The Central Convent*, pp. 448–49, 659–61. For other examples of papal interference, see Vogel, *Das Recht*, pp. 55–56.

97. Vogel, *Das Recht*, p. 147. See also *The Catalan Rule*, p. 38.

98. *Conciliae Magni Britannie* 2.351, 380–81. The references date from after 1291, but the practice is already apparent in 1260. See *Monumentorum Boicorum*, pp. 197–202.

99. Riley-Smith, "The Structures," pp. 136–39; Vogel, *Das Recht*, pp. 147, 261, 308–9.

100. Vogel, *Das Recht*, p. 308, drawing on an earlier suggestion by Burgtorf.

101. Burgtorf, *The Central Convent*, pp. 113–14.

102. *Cart Hosp* 2.863.

103. *Cart Hosp* 2.31–40; Riley-Smith, *The Knights of St John*, pp. 293–95.

104. Burgtorf, *The Central Convent*, pp. 115–21.

105. Burgtorf, *The Central Convent*, pp. 191–92.

106. Luttrell, "The Hospitallers' Early Written Records," pp. 136, 143–46, 151.

107. Riley-Smith, *The Knights of St John*, pp. 293–95; Riley-Smith, "The Structures," pp. 135–36.

108. See *Cart Hosp* 1.138–39, 189, 222, 272–73.

109. *Papsturkunden für Templer und Johanniter* 2.225.

110. See *Cart Hosp* 2.33, 553–54; Riley-Smith, *The Knights of St John*, p. 287. See *Cart Hosp* 3.137–38 for a dispensation for a very elderly man from the arduous crossing of the Mediterranean.

111. William of Santo Stefano, "Recueil," ff. 263–64. See Burgtorf, *The Central Convent*, pp. 245–338; Riley-Smith, *The Knights of St John*, pp. 304–40; Barber, *The New Knighthood*, pp. 188–90; Demurger, *Les Templiers*, pp. 145–47; Claverie, *L'Ordre du Temple en Terre Sainte* 1.109–25.

112. *Cart Hosp* 3.31, 33, 58–60; *Documenti inediti*, ed. Belgrano, p. 60; Mas Latrie, *Histoire de l'île de Chypre* 3.665; *Règle du Temple*, pp. 325, 326; Schottmüller, *Der Untergang* 2.135. See Claverie, *L'Ordre du Temple en Terre Sainte* 1.120–21. The Templar commander of Acre, although technically not a capitu-

lar bailiff, held a significant post, which was occupied by a succession of senior knights, including the future grand masters Renaud of Vichier and Thibault Gaudini.

113. Riley-Smith, *The Knights of St John*, p. 321.

114. Burgtorf, *The Central Convent*, pp. 406–24.

115. *Règle du Temple*, p. 278. See also Claverie, *L'Ordre du Temple en Terre Sainte* 1.115–16.

116. Riley-Smith, "The Structures," pp. 131–32.

117. Riley-Smith, *The Knights of St John*, p. 311.

118. *Procès* 1.632–34; 2.209–11. Examples of better qualified brothers who remained in Europe include Bernard of Parma, who was received in 1281 and seems to have remained in Italy ("Dei Tempieri e del loro processo in Toscana," pp. 470–78) and Audebert of Portan, who was received in 1276 and lived thereafter in the house at Auxonne, of which he eventually became commander (*Procès* 2.165, 171–72, 349; also perhaps p. 94). For further evidence of this, see Bronstein, *The Hospitallers*, pp. 133–34.

119. See also Forey, "Towards a Profile," pp. 200–201.

120. For example Hugh of Bethsan, who may have been from one of the seigneurial families in Palestine. Emile G. Léonard, *Introduction au cartulaire manuscrit du Temple (1150–1317), constitué par le marquis d'Albon et conserve à la Bibliothèque nationale, suivie d'un tableau des maisons françaises du Temple et de leurs precepteurs* (Paris, 1930), p. 25; "Fragment d'un cartulaire de Saint Lazare," p. 128. For the family of Bethsan, see *Lignages d'Outremer*, ed. Marie-Adélaïde Nielen (Paris, 2003), pp. 109–19 and passim; Emmanuel G. Rey, *Les Familles d'Outre-mer de Du Cange* (Paris, 1869), pp. 248–56. Others were Hugh Geoffrey (Léonard, *Introduction*, pp. 24, 89; *Documenti sulle relazioni*, p. 27; Hans Mayer, *Marseilles Levantehandel und ein akkonensisches Fälscheratelier des 13. Jahrhunderts* [Tübingen, 1972], p. 183), Peter Iterius (Léonard, *Introduction*, p. 40; *Documenti sulle relazioni*, p. 27; Mayer, *Marseilles Levantehandel*, p. 183) and William Arnaud (Léonard, *Introduction*, pp. 53, 62; *Cart Hosp* 2.463).

121. Burgtorf, *The Central Convent*, pp. 506–7, 612–13.

122. It was believed as late as the seventeenth century that the brothers had originally been divided into the discrete categories of priests, nurses, and armsbearers; Goussancourt, *Le Martyrologie* 2.112.

123. Burgtorf, *The Central Convent*, p. 423.

124. For example, the Templars Gilbert Alboin (*Les Archives*, ed. Delaville Le Roulx, p. 183; Léonard, *Introduction*, p. 107), Guy of Aubon (*Cart Hosp* 3.31, 33, 58, 60; Léonard, *Introduction*, p. 156), Bartholomew Bocheri (*Procès* 2.191–95), William of Torrage, although he was thirty-five years old and a widower when he entered the order (*Procès* 2.11–12), and Thomas of Stanford (*Conciliae Magni Britannie* 2.344, 365, 366, 367, 372). William of Errée, who was received in ca. 1259, was in Acre in the 1270s, but was back in the commandery of Laumagne

by the mid 1280s (*Procès* 2.13–15). William Aprilis, who was received at Barletta in c.1276, spent only seven years in the east (*Procès* 2.236–8).

125. *Procès* 2.138, 144–5, 147–8, 153, 157, 259; *Le procès des Templiers d'Auvergne*, ed. Sève, pp. 118, 146, 186–7, 220; Mas Latrie, *Histoire de l'île de Chypre* 3.665; Léonard, *Introduction*, p. 72.

126. Arnald of Miserata, Bermond of Luzancion, Raymond of Aiguille, and Ximenes of Labata; Bronstein, *The Hospitallers*, pp. 133–35, and for the details of their careers, pp. 156–57, 163, 165.

127. Bulst-Thiele, *Sacrae Domus*, pp. 217–18.

128. *Procès*, passim; "Inquesta," ed. Frale, pp. 206–10; Léonard, *Introduction*, pp. 17–19, 20, 115, 150–51, 154. For the mastership election, see *Procès* 2.224–25. For its date, see the letter from James of Molay in Forey, *The Templars in the Corona de Aragón*, pp. 405–6.

129. Riley-Smith, *The Knights of St John*, pp. 280–82. Burgtorf (*The Central Convent*, pp. 510–11) is inclined to believe, however, that there were two Ferrands.

130. See Demurger, *Les Templiers*, pp. 132–34. For the general topic of motivation, see Carraz, *L'ordre du Temple*, pp. 291–96, 405–17. Dr Jochen Schenk's study of the relationships between local families and commanderies in Champagne and Languedoc has still to be published.

131. Carraz, *L'ordre du Temple*, pp. 291–96, 299.

132. *Procès* 2.152. For Franco, see *Procès* 1.233, 416, 513, 602, 605, 611; 2.7, 149, 152, 221, 228, 255, 280, 324; *Le procès des Templiers d'Auvergne*, ed. Sève, pp. 140, 146–47, 163, 175, 202, 221, 224, 229, 234, 238; Schottmüller, *Der Untergang* 2.18; Finke, *Papsttum* 2.316, 353; *Monumentorum Boicorum*, p. 198. Léonard, *Introduction*, pp. 17, 96, 161, 165–66, 172.

133. *Procès* 2.362; "Inquesta," ed. Frale, p. 206. For the first Humbert, see Léonard, *Introduction*, pp. 16, 96, 114, 132.

134. Burgtorf, *The Central Convent*, pp. 429, 625.

135. *Procès* 1.204.

136. *Procès* 2.138, 143; *Le procès des Templiers d'Auvergne*, ed. Sève, pp. 143–44.

137. *Procès* 1.471; 2.77, 322–23, 353, 390.

138. *Procès* 1.241, 243, 460, 468, 475.

139. Burgtorf, *The Central Convent*, pp. 694–95.

140. Burgtorf, *The Central Convent*, p. 683.

141. Burgtorf, *The Central Convent*, pp. 620–21.

142. Burgtorf, *The Central Convent*, p. 595.

143. Riley-Smith, *The Knights of St John*, p. 209; Burgtorf, *The Central Convent*, pp. 428–29.

144. Burgtorf, *The Central Convent*, pp. 429, 585–87.

145. Burgtorf, *The Central Convent*, p. 428.

146. Alain Demurger, *Jacques de Molay: Le crepuscule des Templiers* (Paris, 2002), p. 50.

147. Demurger, *Jacques de Molay*, p. 50.

148. Bulst-Thiele, *Sacrae Domus*, pp. 30–31, 126–27; Riley-Smith, *The First Crusaders*, pp. 101–2.

149. See Constance Bouchard, *Sword, Miter and Cloister* (Ithaca, 1987), pp. 292–95; Wilhelm Karl zu Isenburg, Frank Freytag von Loringhoven, et al., *Europäische Stammtafeln*, 2nd ed., 25 vols so far (Marburg and Berlin, 1980–), 11.156; Bulst-Thiele, *Sacrae Domus*, pp. 259–60; Jonathan Riley-Smith, "Family Traditions and Participation in the Second Crusade," *The Second Crusade and the Cistercians*, ed. Michael Gervers (New York, 1992), p. 104.

150. Carraz, *L'ordre du Temple*, pp. 71–72, 79, 299, 307, 309, 320–22, 408, 449, 454, 458, 475.

151. See Bronstein, *The Hospitallers*, pp. 133–36.

152. Robert Burgundio of Craon, Everard of Barres, Bernard of Tremelay, Andrew of Montbard, Robert of Sablé, William of Chartres, William of Beaujeu, and James of Molay.

153. William and Fulk of Villaret.

Four   Two Very Different Orders

1. *Vitae paparum Avenionensium*, ed. Etienne Baluze and Guillaume Mollat, 4 vols (Paris, 1914–27), 3.151.

2. Gustave Schlumberger, Ferdinand Chalandon, and Adrien Blanchet, *Sigillographie de l'Orient latin* (Paris, 1943), p. 250.

3. *Règle du Temple*, p. 340.

4. *Cart Hosp* 2.557. The knight Galius in Acre, who professed in 1155 and may well have become a brother-at-arms, was described by the wife he had left for the order as "frater et humilis servus pauperum Iherusalem"; *Cart Hosp* 1.179.

5. Elm, *Umbilicus Mundi*, pp. 498–506; Vogel, *Das Recht*, pp. 229–33.

6. Bartholomew Cotton, *Historia Anglicana*, ed. Henry R. Luard, Rolls Series 16 (London, 1859), pp. 203–4; also *Cart Hosp* 3.597–98. See Forey, "The Military Orders in the Crusading Proposals," pp. 321–22.

7. See *Councils and Synods, with Other Documents Relating to the English Church*, vol 2 ed. F. Maurice Powicke and Christopher R. Cheney (Oxford, 1964), pp. 1112–13 (for Canterbury); *Sacrorum Conciliorum Nova et Amplissima Collectio*, ed. Giovan Domenico Mansi, 31 vols (Florence and Venice, 1759–98), 24.1079 (for Milan); Eberhard of Regensburg, "Annales," *MGHS* 17.594 (for Salzburg); John of Tielrode, "Chronicon Sancti Bavonis," *MGHS* 25.581–82 (for Rheims

and Sens). The performance of the Hospital was questioned again at the council of Vienne in 1311–12, when the disposal of the Templars' estates was debated. See especially Finke, *Papsttum* 2.260, 281–85, 294–302. For the decision, see *Conciliorum Oecumenicorum Decreta*, ed. J. Alberigo et al. (Freiburg, 1962), pp. 320–36.

8. Luttrell, "The Hospitallers' Early Written Records," pp. 138–39. For the Templar archive, see above, p. 3 and 73n15.

9. Nicholas III, *Les Registres*, ed. Jules Gay and Suzanne Vitte (Paris, 1898–1938), p. 51. For later criticism see John of Tielrode, "Chronicon," p. 581. In the aftermath of the fall of Acre the Hospitallers decided that the complement of brothers-at-arms in the convent at Limassol should be only forty knights and ten sergeants: less than the number they envisaged garrisoning Crac des Chevaliers only half a century before; Anthony Luttrell, "Gli Ospitalieri di San Giovanni di Gerusalemme dal Continente alle Isole," *Acri 1291: La fine della presenza degli ordini militari in Terra Santa e i nuovi orientamenti nel XIV secolo*, ed. Francesco Tommasi (Perugia, 1996), p. 80.

10. There was a reference to the Hospitallers' acts of charity in Pope Clement V's bull, which transferred the Templar estates to them; *Conciliorum Oecumenicorum Decreta*, p. 320. But it was being said, obviously inaccurately, that Pope Clement V finally decided in favor of them when he heard the news of a major engagement, in which they lost seventy-five brethren and the Turks fifteen hundred soldiers. Finke, *Papsttum* 2.299. A comment in a report to the king of Aragon, who was strongly opposed to the transference of Templar properties in his kingdom to the Hospitallers, that the Hospital should not be entrusted with the Templar goods because it managed its own endowment so badly, "making beautiful rooms and palaces rather than confronting the enemies of the faith" may have masked a reference to its hospitals; Finke, *Papsttum* 2.260.

11. Jacquemart Gielee, *Renart le Nouvel*, pp. 302–10. See also Nicholson, *Templars, Hospitallers and Teutonic Knights*, pp. 73–74.

Epilogue

1. William of Santo Stefano's collected works are to be found in Rome, Biblioteca Vaticana, Codex Vaticanus Latinus 4852 (his first codex), and Paris, Bibliothèque Nationale, Manuscrits français, Anciens fonds no. 6049. Some extracts have been published. See Riley-Smith, *The Knights of St John*, pp. 272–73; Luttrell, "The Hospitallers' Early Written Records," pp. 139–43; Klement, "Alcune osservazioni," pp. 229–43.

2. William of Santo Stefano, "Comment la sainte maison de l'Hospital de S. Johan de Jerusalem commença," *RHC Oc* 5.424.

3. Karen Liebreich, *Fallen Order* (London, 2004 pbk edn.), p. 232.

4. Riley-Smith, "Were the Templars Guilty?" pp. 107–24; Frale, *I Templari,* pp. 140–44, 153. Demurger (*Les Templiers,* pp. 484–509) sits on the fence.

5. See Riley-Smith, "The Origins of the Commandery," pp. 15–16.

6. Riley-Smith, "The Structures," pp. 125–43.

7. See Udo Arnold, "Eight Hundred Years of the Teutonic Order," *The Military Orders: Fighting for the Faith and Caring for the Sick,* ed. Malcolm Barber (Aldershot, 1994), pp. 223–32; Udo Arnold and Gerhard Bott, eds., *800 Jahre Deutscher Orden* (Gütersloh and Munich, 1990). For Prussia, see especially Hartmut Boockmann, *Der Deutschen Orden: Zwölf Kapitel aus seiner Geschichte* (Munich, 1981); Norman J. Housley, *The Avignon Papacy and the Crusades, 1305–1378* (Oxford, 1986), pp. 266–81; Norman J. Housley, *The Later Crusades, 1274–1580: From Lyons to Alcazar* (Oxford, 1992), pp. 322–75; Werner Paravicini, *Die Preussenreise des Europäischen Adels,* 2 vols (Sigmaringen, 1989–95); Axel Ehlers, *Die Ablasspraxis des Deutschen Ordens im Mittelalter* (Marburg, 2007).

8. See Bonneaud, *Le prieuré de Catalogne*; Anthony Luttrell, *The Hospitallers in Cyprus, Rhodes, Greece and the West (1291–1440)* (Aldershot, 1978); Anthony Luttrell, *Latin Greece, the Hospitallers and the Crusades, 1291–1400* (Aldershot, 1982); Anthony Luttrell, *The Hospitallers of Rhodes and their Mediterranean World* (Aldershot, 1992); Anthony Luttrell, *The Hospitaller State on Rhodes and Its Western Provinces, 1306–1462* (Aldershot, 1999); Luttrell, *The Town of Rhodes*; Jürgen Sarnowsky, *Macht und Herrschaft im Johanniterorden des 15. Jahrhunderts: Verfassung und Verwaltung der Johanniter auf Rhodos (1421–1522)* (Münster, 2001); Nicolas Vatin, *L'Ordre de Saint-Jean-de-Jérusalem, l'Empire Ottoman et la Méditerranée orientale entre les deux sièges de Rhodes (1480–1522)* (Paris, 1994); O'Malley, *The Knights Hospitaller.*

9. See Blondy, *L'Ordre de Malte*; J. Quentin Hughes, *The Building of Malta* (London, 1956); Stanley Fiorini and Victor Mallia-Milanes, eds., *Malta: A Case Study in International Cross-Currents* (Malta, 1991); Victor Mallia-Milanes, ed., *Hospitaller Malta 1530–1798* (Msida, 1993); David Allen, "The Order of St John as a 'School for Ambassadors' in Counter-Reformation Europe," *The Military Orders,* vol 2, *Welfare and Warfare,* ed. Helen Nicholson (Aldershot, 1998), pp. 326–79.

10. Riley-Smith, *The Knights of St John,* p. 198.

11. Luttrell, *The Town of Rhodes,* pp. 99–100. See Luttrell, "The Hospitallers' Medical Tradition," pp. 68–81; Fotini Karassava-Tsilingiri, "The Fifteenth-Century Hospital of Rhodes," *The Military Orders: Fighting for the Faith and Caring for the Sick,* ed. Malcolm Barber (Aldershot, 1994), pp. 89–96; Ann Williams, "*Xenodochium* to Sacred Infirmary," *The Military Orders: Fighting for the Faith and Caring for the Sick,* ed. Malcolm Barber (Aldershot, 1994), pp. 97–102.

12. Luttrell, "The Military Orders, 1312–1798," p. 343.

13. Luttrell, "The Hospitallers' Medical Tradition," pp. 80–81; Blondy, *L'Ordre de Malte*, pp. 42–44; Roger Ellul Micallef, "The Maltese Medical Tradition," *Malta: A Case Study in International Cross-Currents*, ed. Stanley Fiorini and Victor Mallia-Milanes (Malta, 1991), pp. 188–94.

14. Henry Sire, *The Knights of Malta* (New Haven and London, 1994), pp. 251–53; Maximilian Freiherr von Twickel, "Die nationalen Assoziationen des Malteser-ordens in Deutschland," *Der Johanniterorden, Der Malteserorden*, ed. Adam Wienand (Cologne, 1970), pp. 471–78.

BIBLIOGRAPHY

Manuscript Sources

William Caoursin. *Obsidionis Rhodiae urbis descriptio* (1480), Bibl. Nat. Ms. Lat. 6067.
William of Santo Stefano. "Recueil," Bibl. Nat. Ms. fr. Anciens fonds no. 6049.

Primary Sources

Acta Sanctorum quotquot toto orbe coluntur, ed. Société des Bollandistes, 70 vols so far (Antwerp, Brussels, Tongerloe, 1643–).
"Administrative Regulations for the Hospital of St John in Jerusalem dating from the 1180s," ed. Susan Edgington, *Crusades* 4 (2005).
"Annales de Terre Sainte," ed. Reinhold Röhricht and Gaston Raynaud, *AOL* 2 (1884).
"Annales monasterii Burtonensis," ed. Henry R. Luard, *Annales Monastici*, 5 vols. Rolls Series 36 (London, 1864–69).
Les Archives, la bibliothèque et le trésor de l'ordre de Saint-Jean de Jérusalem à Malte, ed. Joseph Delaville Le Roulx (Paris, 1883).
Ayyubids, Mamlukes and Crusaders: Selections from the Tarikh al-Duwal wa'l Muluk of Ibn al-Furat, ed. Ursula Lyons and Malcolm Lyons, with notes by Jonathan Riley-Smith, 2 vols (Cambridge, 1971).
Bartholomew Cotton. *Historia Anglicana*, ed. Henry R. Luard. Rolls Series 16 (London, 1859).
Benjamin of Tudela. *Itinerary*, ed. and tr. Marcus N. Adler (London, 1907).
Bernard of Clairvaux. "De laude novae militiae ad milites Templi liber," *Sancti Bernardi Opera*, ed. Jean Leclercq et al., 8 vols (Rome, 1963).

Biblioteca Bio-Bibliografica della Terra Santa e dell'Oriente Francescano, comp. Girolamo Gulobovich, 18 vols (Florence, 1906–48).

Bullarium Franciscanum, Romanorum Pontificum Constitutiones, Epistolas, ac Diplomata, ed. Giovanni Giacinto Sbaralea et al., 7 vols (Rome, 1758–1904).

Le Cartulaire du chapitre du Saint-Sépulcre de Jérusalem, ed. Geneviève Bresc-Bautier (Paris, 1984).

Cartulaire général de l'ordre des Hospitaliers de S. Jean de Jérusalem (1100–1310), ed. Joseph Delaville Le Roulx, 4 vols (Paris, 1894–1906).

Cartulaires des Templiers de Douzens, ed. Pierre Gérard and Elisabeth Magnou (Paris, 1965).

The Catalan Rule of the Templars, ed. Judith Upton-Ward (Woodbridge, 2003).

"Chartes d'Adam, abbé de Notre-Dame du Mont-Sion, concernant Gerard, éveque de Valanea, et le prieuré de Saint-Samson d'Orleans (1289)," ed. Alexandre Bruel, *ROL* 10 (1903–4).

"Chartes de Terre Sainte," ed. Joseph Delaville Le Roulx, *ROL* 11 (1905–8).

"Les Chemins et les Pelerinages de la Terre Sainte," ed. Henri Michelant and Gaston Raynaud, *Itinéraires à Jérusalem et descriptions de la Terre Sainte rédigés en français* (Geneva, 1882).

Codice diplomatico del sacro militare ordine Gerosolimitano oggi di Malta, ed. Sebastiano Paoli, 2 vols (Lucca, 1733–37).

"Le Comté de Tripoli dans les chartes du fonds des Porcellets," ed. Jean Richard, *Bibliothèque de l'Ecole des Chartes* 130 (1972).

Conciliae Magni Britannie et Hibernie, ed. David Wilkins, 3 vols (London, 1737).

Conciliorum Oecumenicorum Decreta, ed. J. Alberigo et al. (Freiburg, 1962).

La continuation de Guillaume de Tyr (1184–97), ed. M. Ruth Morgan (Paris, 1982).

Councils and Synods, with Other Documents Relating to the English Church, vol 2, ed. F. Maurice Powicke and Christopher R. Cheney (Oxford, 1964).

De constructione castri Saphet, ed. Robert Huygens (Amsterdam, 1981).

"Dei Tempieri e del loro processo in Toscana," ed. Telesforo Bini, *Atti della Reale Accademia Lucchese di Scienze, Lettere ed Arti* 13 (1845).

Documenti inediti reguardanti le due crociate di San Ludovico IX re di Francia, ed. Luigi Belgrano (Genoa, 1859).

Documenti sulle relazioni delle città toscane coll'Oriente cristiano e coi Turchi fino all'anno 1531, ed. Giuseppe Müller. Documenti degli archivi toscani 3 (Florence, 1879).

Early Mamluk Diplomacy (1260–1290): Treaties of Baybars and Qalawun with Christian Rulers, trans. Peter M. Holt (Leiden, 1995).

Eberhard of Regensburg. "Annales," *MGHS* 17.

"Ein unbekanntes Privileg Fürst Bohemonds II für das Hospital," ed. Rudolf Hiestand, *Archiv für Diplomatik* 43 (1997).

Ernoul. "L'Estat de la Cité de Iherusalem," ed. Henri Michelant and Gaston Raynaud, *Itinéraires à Jérusalem et descriptions de la Terre Sainte rédigés en français* (Geneva, 1882).

"L'Estoire de Eracles," *RHC Oc* 2.

"Exordium Hospitalariorum," *RHC Oc* 5.

Fidenzio of Padua. "Liber recuperationis Terrae Sanctae," ed. Girolamo Gulobovich, *Biblioteca Bio-Bibliografica della Terra Santa e dell'Oriente Francescano*, 18 vols (Florence, 1906–48).

Finke, Heinrich. *Papsttum und Untergang des Templerordens*, 2 vols (Berlin, 1907).

Fita y Colomé, Fidel. *Siete concilios españoles* (Madrid, 1882).

Flores historiarum, ed. Henry R. Luard, 3 vols. Rolls Series 95 (London, 1890).

"Fragment d'un cartulaire de l'ordre de Saint Lazare en Terre-Sainte," ed. Arthur de Marsy, *AOL* 2 (1884).

Goussancourt, Mathieu de. *Le Martyrologie des Chevaliers de St Jean de Jérusalem*, 2 vols (Paris, 1643).

"Hugh Peccator," ed. Jean Leclercq, "Un document sur les débuts des Templiers," *Revue d'histoire ecclésiastique* 52 (1957).

"L'inedito processso del Templari in Castiglia (Medina del Campo, 27 Aprile 1310)," ed. Josep Maria Sans i Travé, *Acri 1291: Le fine della presenza degli ordini militari in Terra Santa e i nuovi orientamenti nel XIV secolo*, ed. Francesco Tommasi (Perugia, 1996).

Innocent III. *Die Register*, ed. Othmar Hageneder et al., 7 vols so far (Graz/Cologne/Rome/Vienna, 1964–).

Innocent III. "Register," *PL* 214–16.

"Inquesta dominorum Commissariorum Clementis pape in Castro de Caynone diocesis Turonensis," ed. Barbara Frale, *Il papato e il processo ai Templari: L'inedita assoluzione di Chinon alla luce della diplomatica pontificia* (Rome, 2003).

"Interrogatorio di Templari in Cesena (1310)," ed. Francesco Tommasi, *Acri 1291: Le fine della presenza degli ordini militari in Terra Santa e i nuovi orientamenti nel XIV secolo*, ed. Francesco Tommasi (Perugia, 1996).

"Inventaire des pièces de Terre Sainte de l'ordre de l'Hôpital," ed. Joseph Delaville Le Roulx, *ROL* 3 (1895).

"Inventaire et comptes de la succession d'Eudes, comte de Nevers (Acre 1266)," ed. Alphonse-Martial Chazaud, *Mémoires de la société des antiquaires de France*, sér. 4, 2 (1871).

Isaac of l'Etoile. *Sermons*, ed. Anselme Hoste and Gaetano Raciti, 3 vols (Paris, 1967–87).

Jacquemart Gielee. *Renart le Nouvel*, ed. Henri Roussel (Paris, 1961).

James of Vitry. "Historia orientalis seu Hierosolymitana," ed. Jacques Bongars, *Gesta Dei per Francos* (Hannau, 1611).

————. "Sermo XXXVII ad fratres ordinis militaris, insignitos charactere Militiae Christi," ed. Jean-Baptiste Pitra, *Analecta Novissima Spicilegii Solesmensis Altera Continuatio*, 2 vols (Paris, 1885–88).

————. "Sermo XXXVIII ad fratres ordinis militaris," ed. Jean-Baptiste Pitra, *Analecta Novissima Spicilegii Solesmensis Altera Continuatio*, 2 vols (Paris, 1885–88).

Javierre Mur, Aurea. "Aportacion al estudio del proceso contra el Temple en Castilla," *Revista des Archivos, Bibliotecas y Museos* 69 (1961).

John of Tielrode. "Chronicon Sancti Bavonis," *MGHS* 25.

John of Würzburg. "Peregrinatio," ed. Robert Huygens, *Peregrinationes tres*. CCCM 139 (Turnhout, 1994).

Les Légendes de l'Hôpital de Saint-Jean de Jérusalem, ed. Antoine Calvet (Paris, 2000).

Lettres des premiers Chartreux, ed. a Carthusian, vol 1 (Paris, 1962).

Lignages d'Outremer, ed. Marie-Adélaïde Nielen (Paris, 2003).

Malteser Urkunden und Regesten zur Geschichte der Tempelherren und der Johanniter, ed. Hans Prutz (Munich, 1883).

Manrique, Angel. *Annales Cistercienses*, 4 vols (Lyons, 1613–59).

Mas Latrie, Louis de. *Histoire de l'île de Chypre sous le règne des princes de la maison de Lusignan*, 3 vols (Paris, 1852–61).

Matthew Paris. *Chronica maiora*, ed. Henry R. Luard, 7 vols, Rolls Series 57 (London, 1872–83).

Mayer, Hans. *Die Kanzlei der lateinischen Könige von Jerusalem*, 2 vols (Hanover, 1996).

————. *Marseilles Levantehandel und ein akkonensisches Fälscheratelier des 13. Jahrhunderts* (Tübingen, 1972).

Menard, Léon. *Histoire civile, ecclésiastique et littéraire de la ville de Nismes*, 7 vols (Paris, 1750).

Monuments historiques relatifs à la condamnation des chevaliers du Temple et à l'abolition de leur ordre, ed. François-Just-Marie Raynouard (Paris, 1813).

Monumentorum Boicorum collectio nova, ed. Accademia scientiarum Boica, 29 ii (Munich, 1831).

"Narratio de primordiis ordinis Theutonici," ed. Max Perlbach, *Die Statuten des Deutschen Ordens* (Halle, 1890).

Nicholas III. *Les Registres*, ed. Jules Gay and Suzanne Vitte (Paris, 1898–1938).

Nicholas IV. *Les Registres*, ed. Ernest Langlois (Paris, 1886–91).

Oliver of Paderborn. *Schriften*, ed. Hermann Hoogeweg (Tübingen, 1894).

"Papst- Kaiser- und Normannenurkunden aus Unteritalien," ed. Walther Holtzmann, *QFIAB* 35 (1955).

Papsturkunden für Kirchen im Heiligen Lande, ed. Rudolf Hiestand. Vorarbeiten zum Oriens Pontificius 3 (Göttingen, 1985).

Papsturkunden für Templer und Johanniter, ed. Rudolf Hiestand, 2 vols. Vorarbeiten zum Oriens Pontificius 2 (Göttingen, 1972–84).

"Pelrinages et pardouns de Acre," ed. Henri Michelant and Gaston Raynaud, *Itinéraires à Jérusalem et descriptions de la Terre Sainte rédigés en français* (Geneva, 1882).

Le procès des Templiers, ed. Jules Michelet, 2 vols (Paris, 1841–51).

Le procès des Templiers d'Auvergne, 1310–1311, ed. Roger Sève and Anne-Marie Chagny-Sève (Paris, 1986).

Prutz, Hans. *Entwicklung und Untergang des Tempelherrenordens* (Berlin, 1888).

Récits d'un ménestral de Reims, ed. Natalis de Wailly (Paris, 1876).

Records of the Templars in England in the Twelfth Century: The Inquest of 1185, ed. Beatrice A. Lees (London, 1935).

Reginald of Durham. *Libellus de Vita et Miraculis S. Godrici, Heremite de Finchale*. Surtees Society 20 (London, 1847).

I registri della cancelleria angioina, ed. Riccardo Filangieri et al., 30 vols (Naples, 1950–71).

La Règle du Temple, ed. Henri de Curzon (Paris, 1886).

Roger of Moulins. "Letter," in Reinhold Röhricht, *Beiträge zur Geschichte der Kreuzzüge*, 2 vols (Berlin, 1874–78).

Rorgo Fretellus of Nazareth. *De locis sanctis terre Jerusalem*, ed. Petrus C. Boeren (Amsterdam, 1980).

Sacrorum Conciliorum Nova et Amplissima Collectio, ed. Giovan Domenico Mansi, 31 vols (Florence and Venice, 1759–98).

Schottmüller, Konrad. *Der Untergang des Templer-Ordens*, 2 vols (Berlin, 1887).

The Synodicum Nicosiense and other Documents of the Latin Church of Cyprus, 1196–1373, ed. Christopher Schabel (Nicosia, 2001).

Tabulae ordinis Theutonici, ed. Ernst Strehlke (Berlin, 1869).

The Templar of Tyre. *Cronaca del Templare di Tiro (1243–1314)*, ed. Laura Minervini (Naples, 2000).

"The Templars and the Castle of Tortosa in Syria," ed. Jonathan Riley-Smith, *English Historical Review* 84 (1969).

Theoderic. "Peregrinatio," ed. Robert Huygens, *Peregrinationes tres*. CCCM 139 (Turnhout, 1994).

Thomas Aquinas. *Summa Theologiae: Opera omnia jussu impensaque Leonis XIII edita*, 4–12 (Rome, 1888–1906).

The Trial of the Templars in the Papal State and the Abruzzi, ed. Anne Gilmour-Bryson (Vatican City, 1982).

Trudon des Ormes, Amedée. "Etude sur les possessions de l'ordre de Temple," *Mémoires de la société des antiquaires de Picardie* 32 (1894).

"A Twelfth-Century Description of the Jerusalem Hospital," ed. Benjamin Kedar, *The Military Orders*, vol 2, *Welfare and Warfare*, ed. Helen Nicholson (Aldershot, 1998).

Die ursprüngliche Templerregel, ed. Gustav Schnürer (Freiburg im Breisgau, 1903).

Vitae paparum Avenionensium, ed. Etienne Baluze and Guillaume Mollat, 4 vols (Paris, 1914–27).

Willbrand of Oldenburg. "Itinerarium Terrae Sanctae," ed. Johann C. M. Laurent, *Peregrinatores medii aevi quatuor,* 2nd ed. (Leipzig, 1873).

William of Santo Stefano. "Comment la sainte maison de l'Hospital de S. Johan de Jerusalem commença," *RHC Oc 5.*

William of Tyre. *Chronicon,* ed. Robert Huygens, 2 parts. CCCM 63, 63A (Turnhout, 1986).

"Zwei unbekannte Diplome der lateinischen Könige von Jerusalem aus Lucca," ed. Rudolf Hiestand, *QFIAB,* 50 (1971).

"Zwei unbekannte Hilfersuchen des Patriarchen Eraclius vor dem Fall Jerusalem (1187)," ed. Nikolas Jaspert, *Deutsches Archiv* 60 (2004).

"Zwei unedierte Texte aus den Kreuzfahrerstaaten," ed. Hans E. Mayer, *Archiv für Diplomatik* 47/48 (2001/2002).

SECONDARY WORKS

Allen, David. "The Order of St John as a 'School for Ambassadors' in Counter-Reformation Europe," *The Military Orders,* vol 2, *Welfare and Warfare,* ed. Helen Nicholson (Aldershot, 1998).

Arnold, Udo. "Eight Hundred Years of the Teutonic Order," *The Military Orders: Fighting for the Faith and Caring for the Sick,* ed. Malcolm Barber (Aldershot, 1994).

Arnold, Udo, and Gerhard Bott, eds. *800 Jahre Deutscher Orden* (Gütersloh and Munich, 1990).

Barbé, Hervé, and Emanuel Damati. "La forteresse médiévale de Safed: Données récentes de l'archéologie," *Crusades* 3 (2004).

Barber, Malcolm. *The New Knighthood: A History of the Order of the Temple* (Cambridge, 1994).

Batiffol, Pierre. Communication in "Correspondence," *Bulletin de la société nationale des antiquaires de France* (1891).

Biffi, Inos. "La figura di Cristo e i "Loca Sancta" nelle vita dei Templari," *I Templari: Una vita tra riti cavallereschi e fedaltà all Chiesa,* ed. Goffredo Viti (Florence, 1995).

Biller, Thomas. "Der Crac des Chevaliers—Neue Forschungen," *Château Gaillard* 20 (2002).

Blondy, Alain. *L'Ordre de Malte au XVIIIe siècle: Des dernières splendeurs à la ruine* (Paris, 2002).

Boas, Adrian. *Archaeology of the Military Orders* (London, 2006).

———. *Jerusalem in the Time of the Crusades* (London and New York, 2001).

———. "Latrun," *Crusades* 4 (2005).

Bonneaud, Pierre. *Le prieuré de Catalogne, le couvent de Rhodes et la couronne d'Aragon 1415–1447* (Millau, 2004).

Boockmann, Hartmut. *Der Deutschen Orden: Zwölf Kapitel aus seiner Geschichte* (Munich 1981).

Bouchard, Constance. *Sword, Miter, and Cloister* (Ithaca, 1987).

Boulton, D'Arcy Jonathan D. *The Knights of the Crown* (Woodbridge, 1987).

Bronstein, Judith. *The Hospitallers and the Holy Land. Financing the Latin East 1187–1274* (Woodbridge, 2005).

Bulst-Thiele, Marie-Luise. *Sacrae Domus Militiae Templi Hierosolymitani Magistri* (Göttingen, 1974).

Burgtorf, Jochen. *The Central Convent of Hospitallers and Templars: History, Organization, and Personnel (1099/1120–1310)* (Leiden and Boston, 2008).

Cahen, Claude. *La Syrie du nord à l'époque des croisades et la principauté franque d'Antioche* (Paris, 1940).

Carraz, Damien. *L'ordre du Temple dans la basse vallée du Rhône, 1124–1312: Ordres militaires, croisades et sociétés méridionales* (Lyon, 2005).

Cerrini, Simonetta. *La Révolution des Templiers* (Paris, 2007).

———, ed. *I Templari, la guerra et la santità* (Rimini, 2000).

———. "La tradition manuscrite de la Règle du Temple," *Autour de la Première Croisade*, ed. Michel Balard (Paris, 1996).

Claverie, Pierre-Vincent. "Les débuts de l'ordre du Temple en Orient," *Le moyen âge* 111 (2005).

———. "L'ordre du Temple au coeur d'une crise politique majeure: La *Querela Cypri* des années 1279–1285," *Le moyen âge* 104 (1998).

———. *L'Ordre du Temple en Terre Sainte et à Chypre au XIIIe siècle*, 3 vols (Nicosia, 2005).

Constable, Giles. "The Place of the Crusader in Medieval Society," *Viator* 29 (1998).

Cottineau, Laurent H. *Répertoire topo-bibliographique des abbayes et prieurés*, 3 vols (Mâcon, 1935–70).

Coureas, Nicholas. *The Latin Church in Cyprus, 1195–1312* (Aldershot, 1997).

Demurger, Alain. *Jacques de Molay: Le crepuscule des Templiers* (Paris, 2002).

———. *Les Templiers: Une chevalerie chrétienne au moyen âge* (Paris, 2005).

Deschamps, Paul. *Les châteaux des croisés en Terre Sainte*, 3 vols (Paris, 1934–77).

Dondi, Cristina. *The Liturgy of the Canons Regular of the Holy Sepulchre of Jerusalem* (Turnhout, 2004).

Edbury, Peter. *The Kingdom of Cyprus and the Crusades, 1191–1374* (Cambridge, 1991).

Edgington, Susan. "Medical Care in the Hospital of St John in Jerusalem," *The Military Orders*, vol 2, *Welfare and Warfare*, ed. Helen Nicholson (Aldershot, 1998).

Edwards, Robert W. "Bağras and Armenian Cilicia: A Reassessment," *Revue des etudes armeniennes* ns 17 (1983).

———. *The Fortifications of Armenian Cilicia* (Washington DC, 1987).

Ehlers, Axel. *Die Ablasspraxis des Deutschen Ordens im Mittelalter* (Marburg, 2007).

Ehlich, M. "The Identification of Emmaus with Abū Gōš Reconsidered," *Zeitschrift des deutschen Palästinavereins* 112 (1996).

Ellenblum, Ronnie. *Crusader Castles and Modern Histories* (Cambridge, 2007).

———. *Frankish Rural Settlement in the Latin Kingdom of Jerusalem* (Cambridge, 1998).

Ellul Micallef, Roger. "The Maltese Medical Tradition," *Malta: A Case Study in International Cross-Currents*, ed. Stanley Fiorini and Victor Mallia-Milanes (Malta, 1991).

Elm, Kaspar. "Kanoniker und Ritter vom Heiligen Grab," *Die geistlichen Ritterorden Europas*, ed. Josef Fleckenstein and Manfred Hellmann (Sigmaringen, 1980).

———. *Umbilicus Mundi* (Sint-Kruis, 1998).

Enlart, Camille. *Les monuments des croisés dans le royaume de Jérusalem: architecture religieuse et civile*, 2 vols and 2 albums (Paris, 1925–28).

Favreau, Marie-Luise. *Studien zur Frühgeschichte des Deutschen Ordens* (Stuttgart, 1975).

Finke, Heinrich. *Papsttum und Untergang des Templerordens*, 2 vols (Berlin, 1907).

Fiorini, Stanley, and Victor Mallia-Milanes, eds. *Malta: A Case Study in International Cross-Currents* (Malta, 1991).

Folda, Jaroslav. *The Art of the Crusaders in the Holy Land, 1098–1187* (Cambridge, 1995).

———. *Crusader Art in the Holy Land from the Third Crusade to the Fall of Acre, 1187–1291* (Cambridge, 2005).

Fonseca, Luis Adão. "As Ordens Militares e a Expansão," *A Alta Nobreza e a Fundação do Estado da Índia* (Lisbon, 2004).

———. "The Portuguese Military Orders and the Oceanic Navigations: From Piracy to Empire," *The Military Orders*, vol 4, *On Land and by Sea*, ed. Judith Upton-Ward (Aldershot, 2008).

———. "La storiografia dell'espansione marittima portoghese (secc. XIV–XV)," *Bullettino dell'Istituto Storico Italiano per il Medio Evo* 106 (2004).

Forey, Alan. *The Fall of the Templars in the Crown of Aragon* (Aldershot, 2001).

———. "Literacy and Learning in the Military Orders during the Twelfth and Thirteenth Centuries," *The Military Orders*, vol 2, *Welfare and Warfare*, ed. Helen Nicholson (Aldershot, 1998).

———. *The Military Orders* (Basingstoke, 1992).

————. "The Military Orders in the Crusading Proposals of the Late-Thirteenth and Early-Fourteenth Centuries," *Traditio* 36 (1980).

————. "Novitiate and Instruction in the Military Orders in the Twelfth and Thirteenth Centuries," *Speculum* 61 (1986).

————. *The Templars in the Corona de Aragón* (London, 1973).

————. "Towards a Profile of the Templars in the Early Fourteenth Century," *The Military Orders: Fighting for the Faith and Caring for the Sick*, ed. Malcolm Barber (Aldershot, 1994).

————. "Women and the Military Orders in the Twelfth and Thirteenth Centuries," repr. in *Hospitaller Women in the Middle Ages*, ed. Anthony Luttrell and Helen Nicholson (Aldershot, 2006).

Frale, Barbara. *I Templari* (Bologna, 2004).

Gervers, Michael. *The Hospitaller Cartulary in the British Library (Cotton MS Nero E VI)* (Toronto, 1981).

————. "Pro defensione Terre Sancte: The Development and Exploitation of the Hospitallers' Landed Estate in Essex," *The Military Orders: Fighting for the Faith and Caring for the Sick*, ed. Malcolm Barber (Aldershot, 1994).

Grégoire, Réginald. "La spiritualità Templare," *I Templari: Una vita tra riti cavallereschi e fedaltà all Chiesa*, ed. Goffredo Viti (Florence, 1995).

Hamilton, Bernard. *The Latin Church in the Crusader States: The Secular Church* (London, 1980).

Harper, Richard P., and Denys Pringle. *Belmont Castle* (Oxford, 2000).

Hiestand, Rudolf. "Die Anfänge der Johanniter," *Die geistlichen Ritterorden Europas*, ed. Josef Fleckenstein and Manfred Hellmann (Sigmaringen, 1980).

————. "*Castrum Peregrinorum* e la fine del dominio crociato in Siria," *Acri 1291: La fine della presenza degli ordini militari in Terra Santa e i nuovi orientamenti nel XIV secolo*, ed. Francesco Tommasi (Perugia, 1996).

————. "Kardinalbischof Matthäus von Albano, das Konzil von Troyes und die Entstehung des Templerordens," *Zeitschrift für Kirchengeschichte* 99 (1988).

————. "Templer- und Johanniterbistümer und -bischöfe im Heiligen Land," *Ritterorden und Kirche im Mittelalter*, ed. Zenon Hubert Nowak. Ordines Militares—Colloquia Torunensia 9 (Torun, 1997).

————. "Zum Problem des Templerzentralarchivs," *Archivalische Zeitschrift* 76 (1980).

Hourlier, Jacques. *L'Age Classique*. Histoire du droit et des institutions de l'église en Occident 10 (Saint-Amand-Montrond, 1974).

Housley, Norman. *The Avignon Papacy and the Crusades, 1305–1378* (Oxford, 1986).

————. *The Later Crusades, 1274–1580: From Lyons to Alcazar* (Oxford, 1992).

Hughes, Quentin. *The Building of Malta* (London, 1956).

Humphreys, R. Stephen. *From Saladin to the Mongols: The Ayyubids of Damascus 1193–1260* (Albany, 1977).

Isenburg, Wilhelm Karl zu, Frank Freytag von Loringhoven, et al. *Europäische Stammtafeln*, 2nd ed., 25 vols so far (Marburg and Berlin, 1980–).

Karassava-Tsilingiri, Fotini. "The Fifteenth-Century Hospital of Rhodes," *The Military Orders: Fighting for the Faith and Caring for the Sick*, ed. Malcolm Barber (Aldershot, 1994).

Kedar, Benjamin. "On the Origins of the Earliest Laws of Frankish Jerusalem: The Canons of the Council of Nablus, 1120," *Speculum* 74 (1999).

Keen, Maurice. *Chivalry* (New Haven and London, 1984).

Klement, Katja. "Alcune osservazioni sul Vat. Lat. 4852," *Studi Melitensi* 3 (1995).

Knöpfler, Alois. "Die Ordensregel der Tempelherren," *Historisches Jahrbuch* 8 (1887).

Knowles, David, and R. Neville Hadcock. *Medieval Religious Houses: England and Wales* (London, 1971).

Legras, Anne-Marie, and Jean-Loup Lemaître. "La pratique liturgique des Templiers et des Hospitaliers de Saint-Jean de Jérusalem," *L'Ecrit dans la société médiévale: Divers aspects de sa pratique du XIe à XVe siècle*, ed. Caroline Bourlet and Annie Dufour (Paris, 1993).

Léonard, Emile G. *Introduction au cartulaire manuscrit du Temple (1150–1317), constitué par le marquis d'Albon et conserve à la Bibliotheque nationale, suivie d'un tableau des maisons françaises du 'Temple et de leurs precepteurs* (Paris, 1930).

Licence, Tom. "The Military Orders as Monastic Orders," *Crusades* 5 (2006).

———. "The Templars and The Hospitallers, Christ and the Saints," *Crusades* 4 (2005).

Liebreich, Karen. *Fallen Order* (London, 2004 pbk edn.).

Lord, Evelyn. *The Knights Templar in Britain* (Harlow, 2004 pbk edn.).

Luttrell, Anthony. "The Earliest Templars," *Autour de la première croisade*, ed. Michel Balard (Paris, 1996).

———. "The Hospitaller Background of the Teutonic Order," *Religiones militares*, ed. Anthony Luttrell and Francesco Tommasi (Città di Castello, 2008).

———. "The Hospitallers' Early Written Records," *The Crusades and their Sources*, ed. John France and William G. Zajac (Aldershot, 1998).

———. *The Hospitallers in Cyprus, Rhodes, Greece and the West (1291–1440)* (Aldershot, 1978).

———. "The Hospitallers' Medical Tradition," *The Military Orders: Fighting for the Faith and Caring for the Sick*, ed. Malcolm Barber (Aldershot, 1994).

———. *The Hospitallers of Rhodes and their Mediterranean World* (Aldershot, 1992).

———. *The Hospitaller State on Rhodes and Its Western Provinces, 1306–1462* (Aldershot, 1999).

———. "Iconography and Historiography: The Italian Hospitallers before 1530," *Sacra Militia* 3 (2002).

————. *Latin Greece, the Hospitallers and the Crusades, 1291–1400* (Aldershot, 1982).

————. "The Military Orders, 1312–1798," *The Oxford Illustrated History of the Crusades*, ed. Jonathan Riley-Smith (Oxford, 1995).

————. "Gli Ospitalieri di San Giovanni di Gerusalemme dal Continente alle Isole," *Acri 1291: La fine della presenza degli ordini militari in Terra Santa e i nuovi orientamenti nel XIV secolo*, ed. Francesco Tommasi (Perugia, 1996).

————. "Préface" to *Les Légendes de l'Hôpital de Saint-Jean de Jérusalem*, ed. Antoine Calvet (Paris, 2000).

————. "The Skull of Blessed Gerard," *The Order's Early Legacy in Malta*, ed. John Azzopardi (Valletta, 1989).

————. "Templari e ospitalieri: alcuni confronti," *I Templari, la guerra e la santità*, ed. Simonetta Cerrini (Rimini, 2000).

————. *The Town of Rhodes, 1306–1356* (Rhodes, 2003).

Luttrell, Anthony, and Helen Nicholson, eds. *Hospitaller Women in the Middle Ages* (Aldershot, 2006).

Luttrell, Anthony, and Léon Pressouyre, eds. *La Commanderie, institution des ordres militaires dans l'Occident médiéval* (Paris, 2002).

Mallia-Milanes, Victor, ed. *Hospitaller Malta 1530–1798* (Msida, 1993).

Marcombe, David. *Leper Knights* (Woodbridge, 2003).

Marshall, Christopher. *Warfare in the Latin East, 1192–1291* (Cambridge, 1992).

Mas Latrie, Louis de. *Histoire de l'île de Chypre sous le règne des princes de la maison de Lusignan*, 3 vols (Paris, 1852–61).

Mayer, Hans. *Die Kanzlei der lateinischen Könige von Jerusalem*, 2 vols (Hanover, 1996).

————. *Marseilles Levantehandel und ein akkonensisches Fälscheratelier des 13. Jahrhunderts* (Tübingen, 1972).

Menard, Léon. *Histoire civile, ecclésiastique et littéraire de la ville de Nismes*, 7 vols (Paris, 1750).

Mitchell, Piers. *Medicine in the Crusades: Warfare, Wounds and the Medieval Surgeon* (Cambridge, 2004).

Nicholson, Helen. *Templars, Hospitallers and Teutonic Knights: Images of the Military Orders 1128–1291* (Leicester 1993).

————. "Women in Templar and Hospitaller Commanderies," *La Commanderie, Institution des ordres militaires dans l'Occident médiéval*, ed. Anthony Luttrell and Léon Pressouyre (Paris, 2002).

O'Malley, Gregory. *The Knights Hospitaller of the English Langue 1460–1565* (Oxford, 2005).

Paravicini, Werner. *Die Preussenreise des Europäischen Adels*, 2 vols (Sigmaringen, 1989–95).

Pringle, Denys. *The Churches of the Crusader Kingdom of Jerusalem: A Corpus*, 4 vols (Cambridge, 1993–2009).

————. *The Red Tower (al-Burj al-Ahmar): Settlement in the Plain of Sharon at the Time of the Crusaders and Mamluks AD 1099–1516* (London, 1986).

————. *Secular Buildings in the Crusader Kingdom of Jerusalem: An Archaeological Gazetteer* (Cambridge, 1997).

Prutz, Hans. *Entwicklung und Untergang des Tempelherrenordens* (Berlin, 1888).

Purkis, William. *Crusading Spirituality in the Holy Land and Iberia, c.1095–c.1187* (Woodbridge, 2008).

Rey, Emmanuel G. *Les Familles d'Outre-mer de Du Cange* (Paris, 1869).

————. *Recherches géographiques et historiques sur la domination des Latins en Orient* (Paris, 1877).

Richard, Jean. "*Cum omni raisagio montanee* . . . A propos de la cession du Crac des Chevaliers aux Hospitaliers," *Itinéraires d'Orient*, ed. Raoul Curiel and Rika Gyselen (Bures-sur-Yvette, 1994).

Riley-Smith, Jonathan. "The Crown of France and Acre, 1254–1291," *France and the Holy Land*, ed. Daniel Weiss and Lisa Mahoney (Baltimore and London, 2004).

————. *The Crusades, Christianity, and Islam* (New York, 2008).

————. "The Death and Burial of Latin Christian Pilgrims to Jerusalem and Acre, 1099–1291," *Crusades* 7 (2008).

————. "Family Traditions and Participation in the Second Crusade," *The Second Crusade and the Cistercians*, ed. Michael Gervers (New York, 1992).

————. *The Feudal Nobility and the Kingdom of Jerusalem, 1174–1277* (London, 1973).

————. *The First Crusade and the Idea of Crusading* (London, 1986).

————. *The First Crusaders, 1095–1131* (Cambridge, 1997).

————. "Further Thoughts on the Layout of the Hospital in Acre," *Chemins d'outre-mer*, ed. Damien Coulon, Catherine Otten-Froux, Paule Pagès, and Dominique Valérien, 2 vols (Paris, 2004).

————. "Guy of Lusignan, the Hospitallers and the Gates of Acre," *Dei gesta per Francos*, ed. Michel Balard, Benjamin Z. Kedar, and Jonathan Riley-Smith (Aldershot, 2001).

————. "An Ignored Meeting of a Templar Chapter-General," *Prof. Dr. Işin Demirkent Anisina*, ed. Abdülkerim Özaydin et al. (Instanbul, 2008).

————. *The Knights of St John in Jerusalem and Cyprus, c. 1050–1310* (London, 1967).

————. "The Military Orders and the East, 1149–1291," *Knighthoods of Christ*, ed. Norman Housley (Aldershot, 2007).

————. "The Origins of the Commandery in the Temple and the Hospital," *La Commanderie, Institution des ordres militaires dans l'Occident médiéval*, ed. Anthony Luttrell and Léon Pressouyre (Paris, 2002).

————. "The Roles of Hospitaller and Templar Sergeants," forthcoming.

————. "The Structures of the Orders of the Temple and the Hospital in c.1291," *Medieval Crusade*, ed. Susan Ridyard (Woodbridge, 2004).

————. "The Templars and the Teutonic Knights in Cilician Armenia," *The Cilician Kingdom of Armenia*, ed. Thomas Boase (Edinburgh, 1978).

————. "Towards a History of the Military-Religious Orders," *The Hospitallers, the Mediterranean and Europe*, ed. Karl Borchardt, Nikolas Jaspert, and Helen Nicholson (Aldershot, 2007).

————. "Were the Templars Guilty?" *Medieval Crusade*, ed. Susan Ridyard (Woodbridge, 2004).

Röhricht, Reinhold. Communication in "Chronique," *ROL* 6 (1898).

Roll, Israel, and Benjamin Arubas. "Le château d'Arsur," *Bulletin monumental* 164 (2006).

Sarnowsky, Jürgen. *Macht und Herrschaft im Johanniterorden des 15. Jahrhunderts: Verfassung und Verwaltung der Johanniter auf Rhodos (1421–1522)* (Münster, 2001).

Scarpellini, Pietro. "La chiesa de San Bevignate, i Templari e la pittura perugina del Duecento," *Templari e Ospitalieri in Italia: La chiesa di San Bevignate in Perugia*, ed. Mario Roncetti, Pietro Scarpellini and Francesco Tommasi (Milan, 1987).

Schlumberger, Gustave, Ferdinand Chalandon, and Adrien Blanchet. *Sigillographie de l'Orient latin* (Paris, 1943).

Schottmüller, Konrad. *Der Untergang des Templer-Ordens*, 2 vols (Berlin, 1887).

Silva, Isabel Morgado S. E., and Maria Cristina Pimenta. "As Ordens de Santiago e de Cristo e a Fundação do Estado da Índia: Uma Perspectiva de Estudo," *A Alta Nobreza e a Fundação do Estado da Índia* (Lisbon, 2004).

Sire, Henry. *The Knights of Malta* (New Haven and London, 1994).

Sloane, Barney, and Gordon Malcolm. *Excavations at the Priory of the Order of the Hospital of St John of Jerusalem, Clerkenwell, London*. MoLAS monograph 20 (London, 2004).

Stern, Edna. "The Hospitaller Order in Acre and Manueth: The Ceramic Evidence," *The Military Orders*, vol 3, *History and Heritage*, ed. Victor Mallia-Milanes (Aldershot, 2008).

Stern, Eliezer. "The Church of St John in Acre," *Crusades* 4 (2005).

————. "La commanderie de l'ordre des Hospitaliers à Acre," *Bulletin monumental* 164 (2006).

Struckmeyer, Myra. "The Sisters of the Order of Saint John at Mynchin Buckland," *Hospitaller Women in the Middle Ages*, ed. Anthony Luttrell and Helen Nicholson (Aldershot, 2006).

Tommasi, Francesco. "Per i rapporti tra Templari e Cistercensi: Orientamenti a indirizzi di ricerca," *I Templari: Una vita tra riti cavallereschi e fedaltà all Chiesa*, ed. Goffredo Viti (Florence, 1995).

Toomaspoeg, Kristjan. *Templari e ospitalieri nella Sicilia medievale* (Taranto, 2003).

Twickel, Maximilian Freiherr von. "Die nationalen Assoziationen des Malteserordens in Deutschland," *Der Johanniterorden, Der Malteserorden*, ed. Adam Wienand (Cologne, 1970).

Upton-Ward, Judith. "The Surrender of Gaston and the Rule of the Templars," *The Military Orders: Fighting for the Faith and Caring for the Sick*, ed. Malcolm Barber (Aldershot, 1994).

Vatin, Nicolas. *L'Ordre de Saint-Jean-de-Jérusalem, l'Empire Ottoman et la Méditerranée orientale entre le deux sièges de Rhodes (1480–1522)* (Paris, 1994).

Vogel, Christian. *Das Recht der Templer* (Münster, 2007).

Williams, Ann. "*Xenodochium* to Sacred Infirmary," *The Military Orders: Fighting for the Faith and Caring for the Sick*, ed. Malcolm Barber (Aldershot, 1994).

INDEX

The names of less well-known locations are followed by their Arabic and, where appropriate, Hebrew equivalents.

JONATHAN RILEY-SMITH

is Dixie Professor of Ecclesiastical History at the University of Cambridge.

He is the author of many influential books and essays, including

The Crusades, Christianity, and Islam.